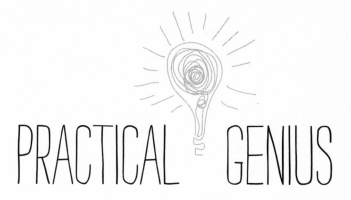

PRACTICAL GENIUS

The Real Smarts You Need to Get
Your Talents and Passions Working for YOU

GINA AMARO RUDAN

A Touchstone Book
Published by Simon & Schuster
New York   London   Toronto   Sydney   New Delhi

A Karen Watts Book

Touchstone
A Division of Simon & Schuster, Inc.
1230 Avenue of the Americas
New York, NY 10020

First Touchstone hardcover edition October 2011

TOUCHSTONE and colophon are
registered trademarks of Simon & Schuster, Inc.
A Karen Watts Book (www.karenwattsbooks.com)

For information about special discounts for bulk purchases,
please contact Simon & Schuster Special Sales at 1-866-506-1949
or business@simonandschuster.com.

The Simon & Schuster Speakers Bureau can bring authors to your live event.
For more information or to book an event
contact the Simon & Schuster Speakers Bureau at 866-248-3049
or visit our website at www.simonspeakers.com.

Designed by Ruth Lee-Mui

Manufactured in the United States of America

1   3   5   7   9   10   8   6   4   2

Library of Congress Cataloging-in-Publication Data

Rudan, Gina Amaro.
Practical genius : the real smarts you need to get
your talents and passion working for you / by Gina Amaro Rudan.
p. cm.
1. Self-actualization (Psychology) 2. Genius. 3. Self-perception. 4. Success. I. Title.
BF637.S4R837 2011
158.1—dc22
2011011987

ISBN 978-1-4516-2604-9
ISBN 978-1-4516-2606-3 (ebook)

FOR MY BELOVEDS

My husband, Stephen, whose love and support permeate this book
And for my son, Lucas, whose life is empowered by inventive play and
from whom I learn something amazing every day

CONTENTS

FOREWORD

By Kevin Carroll, speaker, consultant, and author of
Rules of the Red Rubber Ball and *The Red Rubber Ball at Work*

I've been lucky to have known and worked with a lot of geniuses in my life, from the author Paulo Coelho to Cameron Sinclair from Architecture for Humanity to Mel Young, the cofounder of the Homeless World Cup, to Nobel Laureate Archbishop Desmond Tutu. To my mind, these folks are geniuses not for their accomplishments or intelligence, though they are certainly accomplished and crazy intelligent, too. What makes them practical geniuses, as Gina would describe them, is the unique combination of heart and smarts they possess, as committed to the joy, humor, and creativity in their professional lives as they are to excellence in the work they produce. You know one of these geniuses when you see one, believe me.

The first genius I think I ever knew was my great-grandmother Nana Carroll. Nana Carroll was my grandfather's mother. She was mostly Cherokee, and two long, pitch-black braids framed her face and fell past her shoulders. My grandfather Pop-Pop drove my brothers and me to see her every Sunday, each week following the same ritual: the scramble and scuffle to sit by a window; the squeak of the "pleather" of the car seat under my legs; the familiar sights and sounds and smells that came through the window all the way to Brook Street in Bryn Mawr, Pennsylvania, where Nana Carroll lived.

As much as I loved the ride to Brook Street, it always turned to dread as we got close to Nana Carroll's house. I knew she would be waiting for us, sitting in the rocking chair in her bedroom listening for us to thump up the stairs to say hello. Then, after giving us each a kiss, she'd impose what felt like a life sentence on us, sweetly but firmly saying "It's good to see you boys again. Now, before you go outside to play I need you to be still for five minutes." Be still. For five minutes. Three hundred seconds, to be precise. A lifetime to a grade-school-aged boy with ants in his pants and jumping beans in his pockets and a million shimmering play possibilities beckoning from outside Nana Carroll's bedroom window.

Before I'd enter her room, I'd pray for a pardon from the weekly torment, but it never came. So I'd turn myself over to her, sacrifice my natural state of constant movement for the stillness she demanded.

300 seconds. When I had trouble settling down, she'd gently touch my head or shoulder to soothe me.

245 seconds. A couple more squirms and fidgets, then finally stillness and silence.

215 seconds. I would begin to notice that I could "see" all sorts of things with my ears when I was still. The squeak of the floorboard under Nana Carroll's rocking chair. The clang of a chain-link gate in the neighbor's yard.

180 seconds. Pop-Pop's deep, warm voice telling a sports story to his brothers. The smell of coffee wafting through the cracks in the floor-boards. My brother's stomach growling like an alley cat.

120 seconds. Bikes skidding on street gravel. Cheers from a stickball game that was happening without me. A basketball walloping a make-shift milk crate hoop. To which I could only listen, not respond.

60 seconds. One more long, painful minute of stillness to bear. And when precisely five minutes had passed, Nana Carroll would wave us on to freedom.

It wasn't until I was much older that I realized the genius of this ritual. She wasn't torturing us, she was sharing a very sacred and common Native American practice that she knew would be valuable to us as we gained life experience. She was passing on a gift of her genius, the art and power of being exactly in the moment and nowhere else—and the secret of awareness and discovery that could be found in stillness.

Gina's book, *Practical Genius,* brought back powerful memories of this lesson, how it took root in me and shaped the way I live and work and play in the world. "We all have our very own innate genius, an intellectual sweet spot located somewhere between our heart and mind," Gina writes.

I live at that sweet spot, thanks in part to Nana Carroll sharing her genius with me. Be still now, and begin the journey of *Practical Genius* that will show you how to live in yours, too.

Kevin Carroll
www.kevincarrollkatalyst.com

PRACTICAL GENIUS

A SPARK OF GENIUS

Where the Journey Begins

Do you ever feel as though you are two separate people—the face you present at the office and the authentic self you are in the rest of your life?

Do you feel as though there's a whole set of your skills, talents, and assets that you're not using every day because you've allowed what you do for a living to become what you are?

So many of us wake up every day to a dreaded alarm clock that drags us from the comfort of our cozy beds to pitch us into daily routines—routines that we have willingly chosen but often can't quite remember why. Many of us go to jobs, earn a living, maybe we're even doing what we are good at for eight hours a day (or more).

But most likely we're not doing what we love. We march through the stages of life—college, career, marriage, kids, more career—and we wake up one day and twenty or thirty years have passed, and we wonder, "Hey, what was that? What do I have to show for it? Who *am* I?"

How do smart, motivated, accomplished people like us, who are walking around with all the human assets one could ever hope for, end up in this no-man's-land? How did we fool ourselves into believing that this was the best we could do?

THE DE-GENIUSED SELF

The great American engineer and futurist Buckminster Fuller once said, "Everyone is born a genius, but the process of living de-geniuses you." That's a fact, Jack, and it's why we have two types of problems:

Problem A

You're going through the motions, armed with the latest technology and a closet full of career wear, and you're thinking "This is okay, I've got a good life" while ignoring the fact that there is a whole other side of you that lies dormant, eager to be released from the tidy cage of your conformity. You are one of the millions battling with the Dr. Jekyll and Mr. Hyde syndrome, checking half of yourself at the revolving doors of your office building, walking through your workday with an unconvincing smile, sitting silently in one too many meetings doodling a masterpiece in your Moleskine notebook.

If this sounds like you, you have allowed yourself to be de-geniused.

Problem B

You're a die-hard creative person working from a home studio, swimming though life with the imaginative right side of your brain leading the way while the practical left side is unactivated. You pass your days, months, and years waiting patiently for a "lucky break." You bounce from inspiration to inspiration, passionately invested in the creative process but not in the *business* of being creative.

If this is who you see in the mirror every day, you, too, have allowed yourself to be de-geniused.

So many of us are unconsciously compromising some of our greatest natural assets because of external factors, past hurts, or current fears. Or, even worse, we have sacrificed our skills, strengths, and passion to the expectations and influence of others. Or we're consciously hitting the snooze button, rolling over and going back to sleep every time we're reminded how far from feeling happy and fulfilled we are in our work and personal lives.

I call this the "de-geniused self," and he has been allowed to sit in the driver's seat of our lives for far too long. The de-geniused self sabotages your potential, holds you back, and accepts mediocrity. This is the side of you that operates from fear and shines dimly, if at all. This is the person who has allowed people, organizations, environments, and circumstances to beat the genius out of you. Enough already!

ARE YOU A GENIUS?

"Will all the geniuses in the room please raise their hands?" I ask this question at every corporate training session I facilitate, and it astonishes me how few hands go up. Regardless of the industry—whether I am speaking to an auditorium full of bankers, marketers, or scientists—most people hesitate, look around to see who else has raised their hands . . . and shyly choose *not* to outwardly demonstrate their belief in their own genius.

If I asked you the question right now, how would you respond? Would you confidently say, "Here I am!" and acknowledge the spark of genius within you? Or would you hesitate and stammer that you're "not so smart, not so special, not really."

The second response was the one I most often received when I first started my Genuine Insights practice, and I must admit it drove the marketer in me crazy. When I discovered how many of my clients had no idea if they even had a drop of genius inside them, I realized I was looking at both a crisis and an opportunity—an opportunity

I seized. So many professionals know exactly what their career strengths and skills are, but the recognition of their most potent ingredients obviously stopped short. Some folks would stare back at me puzzled, not sure how to answer the simple question "What contributes to your genius?" Or they would dismiss the question entirely, not believing it had any relevance to them at all.

I've been studying this concept of "genius" for years now. In that time, I've interviewed hundreds of professionals and asked them for their definition of genius. I've learned that the majority of us have been conditioned to believe that genius is something far beyond our reach. It's amazing how few of us believe we actually possess genius— yet nearly everyone believes it's the secret ingredient of self-fulfillment and success in life and in business.

Let's take Bill, for example. He was a successful investment banker who had been laid off from his firm and decided he wanted to do something completely different with his life and career. During our first session together, I asked Bill what his definition of genius was, and he answered, "Genius is about good genes, and unfortunately, I didn't get any genius genes." In his opinion, genius was an all-or-nothing proposition—either you have it or you don't. Unfortunately, it's an opinion that many of us share.

The problem with the commonly accepted concept of "genius" is that it's a quality—like creativity—that has a magical, elusive connotation. Most people consider genius to be a gift, a lightning bolt from the gods that strikes a lucky few like Mozart or Einstein, but not the rest of us.

I'm here to tell you that this is simply not true. Every one of us has the capacity for genius. Any one of us could achieve or discuss or express something so extraordinary that it could change the world. More important, it could change *your* world.

That doesn't necessarily mean that there's an Isaac Newton or a Leonardo da Vinci deep inside us, just waiting to be discovered.

It means that when you are a fully realized person—authentic and entirely visible to the world—you are capable of exceptional accomplishments in your work, in your community, and among your friends and family.

It means that *you* are the genius, operating not necessarily in the lofty, exclusive heights of science or culture but right here, right now. It's the kind of practical, street-level, everyday genius that can change the game for you, your business, and every aspect of your life.

But if genius is such a game changer, why does the concept of genius seem so alien to our experience? Why have we been programmed to believe that this gorgeous word can be applicable only to a select few who have been blessed with a rare, extraordinary talent?

GENUINE INSIGHT—MY STORY

In 2008, I had one of those life-changing experiences you usually see described on *The Oprah Winfrey Show*. Like more than 20 million people before me, I decided to have corrective eye surgery after having grown tired of wearing glasses or contacts for most of my life. So many people I knew raved about this surgery—you know, "Gina, it's a piece of cake" or "Gina, you will wake up the morning after and will finally be able to see the alarm clock without your glasses."

The stories I *didn't* hear were about the common risks associated with the surgery. I didn't bother to research or investigate them either. I honestly could not be bothered with the details; all I cared about was the end result—no more glasses, no more annoying contacts, nothing but blue sky (that I would be able to see *really, really clearly!*) ahead.

Over the course of the evening after my surgery, I developed an infection. Only one in twenty-five thousand patients gets this particular kind of infection, which results in severe inflammation—and I happened to be one of them. And instead of waking up to that alarm clock experience everyone had predicted, the day after what should have been routine surgery I opened my eyes to . . . nothing. What followed was three days of darkness, certainly the longest three days of my life.

That temporary blindness was as terrifying and painful and deeply disturbing as anything I'd ever experienced. But it also brought the most profound, life-changing insight of my entire life.

The sudden loss of sight placed me in a kind of heightened reality chamber. It was as if I had been given a truth serum, only the truth was being revealed to myself. Though I had very little sight during those days, I could suddenly see one thing very clearly: that I could no longer continue with my traditional job and my existing life.

Not that my working life was so bad. In fact, it was pretty great by most standards. I'd been working in corporate America for more than a decade, rising to great heights in positions at Avon and PR Newswire. I had a great office and nice suits, and I made a healthy salary. From the outside, I looked successful and happy.

But something was missing. While I had been working myself to the bone every day in the office for the last decade, I felt I was hiding a big part of myself—the most important part, my creativity and passion—deep inside. Eventually, I was so stressed out at the prospect of starting my workday that I literally made myself sick. Just about ten months before my scheduled eye surgery, I had been diagnosed with shingles (which, if you've never had it—lucky you).

Shingles is brought on by stress. *How the hell could I end up in the hospital with the shingles over work?* I asked myself at the time. Work that I didn't even love doing anymore. How did this happen? Why? For what reason did I allow myself to get to this miserable moment?

During the days I spent in darkness, I began to see in great detail the actualization of the career I'd always dreamed of, which was to coach and write. Despite this terrifying experience—coupled with the very grim economic reality of the moment (Wall Street had just collapsed, and the rest of the country was rapidly following it down into the sinkhole)—I knew I had to make a dramatic change in my life.

Why did it take darkness for me to see the truth about my life? Saint Paul's similar experience notwithstanding, I can only say that there is tremendous power in the absence of the sensory influences that ordinarily dictate our lives. During my recovery, I was sleeping in the guest room, away from my husband and toddler and away from the world. In the darkness and quiet of those three days, I could see, smell, and taste the future I wanted for myself in a very precise, very detailed way.

During my first night of darkness, I saw myself as a child living my childhood memories. I remember seeing my great-grandmother in a hammock in her wooden home in Arecibo, Puerto Rico. I don't know if it was the meds I was on, a message from God, or just a surreal journey down memory lane, but it was powerful. "If I never see clearly again, at least I have seen my memories," I remember thinking.

On the second evening of darkness, I began to vividly see my future. I saw myself traveling and speaking with large groups of people all over the world. As if I were watching a movie, I saw this character Gina, who was happy, with long moments of quiet, living a life free of anxiety, stress, and that horrible case of shingles that I had only just recovered from right before my eye surgery.

On the third afternoon of my darkness, I listened to dozens of online talks from the influential TED Conference for inspiration, and I realized that what had happened to me was my very own Jill Bolte Taylor "stroke of genius" moment. Do you know Jill Bolte Taylor? She is a renowned brain scientist who found her life turned upside down when she suffered a debilitating stroke in 1996. Her amazing book, *My Stroke of Insight,* recounts her recovery and the insights she gained into the brain's workings from the inside out. The talk she gave about it at the 2008 TED Conference (look it up on TED.com) was phenomenal, and as I listened to her remarkable talk and others that my husband had selected for me, I realized a change was coming. A big change. And I was beginning to see how it was going to happen.

In my dream state, I could feel myself well up with possibility, with a clear image of where I should be, *who* I should be. I knew that what I was seeing represented a radical change for me and my family. The only thing I wasn't seeing yet was how exactly to get there from the dark place on my foldout couch.

But one word kept coming back to me over and over again: genius.

PLAYBOOK

Visualize Your Genuine Insight

This exercise will give you a taste of sightless insight. Find a comfy, private, quiet spot where you will not be interrupted for at least thirty minutes. Set a timer for the amount of time you want to devote to this experience. Close your eyes, or, better, cover them with a scarf. Now lie down and *visualize*. Imagine what a life built on your passions looks like. What do you see? Where are you? Who are you with? What are you wearing? What are you doing with your hands, your feet? What are you saying? When the timer goes off, remove the scarf and write down exactly what you saw with details, lots of details. Note colors, shapes, names, places, activities you were engaged in—all of it. Before you can explore your genius, you have to clearly visualize a life where your passions are front and center, not just daydreamy wishes or hobbies you never got around to enjoying— or, worse yet, ideas that have yet to be born.

REDEFINING GENIUS

I talk a lot about "genius" in this book. What does that word really mean? Read on, because I think you'll find that the definition isn't exactly what you may think.

Traditionally the definition of genius has meant you were gifted with an exceptional skill or talent or a ridiculously high IQ—and if you didn't meet one of these criteria, you were just another ordinary Joe.

Originally derived from the same Latin root as the words "gene" and "genetic," the first definition of genius referred to a spirit given to every person at birth. From there the word "genius" came to mean a spirit in general, as in the fairy-tale "genie" or "jinni." In 1711, Joseph Addison wrote an essay, "On Genius," which was published in *The Spectator* and defined genius as "exceptional talent"—a definition that popularized the word. According to Addison, there were two kinds of genius—natural and learned—and the greatest of geniuses were those *born* with natural talents (compared with others, who had to develop their genius the hard way). He offered William Shakespeare as an example of a "true" genius and Aristotle as an example of someone who merely *learned* to be a genius.

Later, in 1869, Charles Darwin's half cousin Francis Galton the founder of eugenics (meaning "well born") wrote the first social-scientific attempt to define and explain genius. Galton's somewhat arrogant obsession was to improve "the breed of man," and he coined the famous phrase "nature versus nurture."

History's varying definitions of genius all make it sound pretty darn exclusive. If this is to be believed, only 0.1 percent of us are eligible to enjoy the benefits of genius, which means the rest of us miss out. I don't think so!

As you read this book, you are not allowed to think of your IQ score or your SAT score or any other standardized measurement you have locked in your memory. Some people can't remember their mother's home phone number but can tell you on a dime what they scored on their SATs. That's scary. We have given way too much importance to those kinds of numbers, but that's for someone else's book to debunk. My quest is not to bash the standardized testing industry but to reprogram you to consider a new approach to identifying and cultivating your genius. And not the $E = mc^2$ kind of genius, but the kind that sparks to life of your own volition.

Many of us do not live up to our potential simply because of insufficient motivation or belief in our own powers. Others fail due to adults' inattention to our potential in childhood. And when someone is granted the title "genius," he is then motivated to perform at his highest ability and granted greater trust in his mastery. Think about how your life would have changed if as a child your natural genius had been acknowledged and nurtured and been the core of your personal development. Instead, traditional education prioritizes standardized tests as the measure for intelligence and aptitude, and as a result we have been holding ourselves back for centuries.

Imagine how the world would be if everyone believed they had a spark of genius within them. Individuals, communities, even whole societies would begin to make better, bolder, more confident choices rather than just accepting the status quo. Children would grow up playing with their genius while their parents nurtured it. Schools would be organized differently if we operated from the basis that every child has genius within. Businesses would be able to cultivate genius across the organization rather than for only a select few.

Everyday geniuses can be found on campuses, within corporations, and on playing fields around the world. Some are teachers, at-home moms, or executives who focus on doing things their way. Take Ursula Mejia-Melgar, who had a passion for an unusual combination: food and chemistry. Instead of ignoring either her strength as a scientist or her creative passion for food, Ursula married them with great ingenuity and energy, and the result is a kick-ass career with General Mills, a giant corporation that believes in both sides of Ursula and recently sent her on her first long-term international assignment to Switzerland to work on a innovative partnership with Nestlé.

Or look at Brian Bordainick, a twenty-five-year-old teacher in the Ninth Ward of New Orleans who began his career during the immediate post-Katrina era and decided to set out to do the impossible: build a football sports stadium with zero funds and a fierce determination. His mission was to get kids off the streets and give them a field to play and dream in. Brian set his young mind on a "field of dreams" and succeeded in raising $2.5 million in less than two years, after most people said he would never be able to pull it off. The stadium is being built at the time of this writing.

Ursula and Brian are people who are leveraging their skills right alongside their values and passions and changing people's minds about what is possible. They both innately operate from a genius zone and do not compromise one side of themselves for another.

Every genius thinker looks at what someone else is looking at and sees something different. When I consider the contemporary notion of genius, I see something different, too. So let's begin by taking back the word and redefining it in a practical way. No more lofty, fancy, scientific definitions, visuals, or preconceived notions allowed. I want you to let go of that limited, flawed definition of genius and acknowledge that we possess the ability to discover what I call "practical genius." In fact, we all have our very own innate genius, an intellectual sweet spot located somewhere between our heart and mind. As you read this book, you will discover how to find that sweet spot and maximize the returns on your most precious capital—your Practical Genius.

This book will challenge you to think, act, and measure your abilities in a different way than anyone has ever asked you to before. The changes I am suggesting will be directed toward improving yourself, your existing ideas, and how you go about sharing them with the world. When you do that, you will be able to develop better programs and products. You will be able to change companies and communities. You will be able to improve schools, have better relationships, and ultimately become an entirely transformed professional and person. Rather than continue to channel your abilities toward the narrowest of purposes, I am going to push you to expand your knowledge, passions, strengths, and creative abilities to levels you may not have known existed within yourself.

If you've spent too many hours wondering exactly what your life's purpose is, please allow yourself a sigh of relief. You have finally picked up a book that will offer you a contemporary, perfectly practical, and deeply meaningful way to answer that question—and do something extraordinary about it.

READY TO GET DOWN TO GENIUS

I knew it was time for me to let go of the nine-to-five and create a new kind of working life—one that would let my own brand of practical genius thrive. And I had a pretty clear vision of what kind of business I wanted to create for myself. Now I needed to put this plan into action.

So on January 1, 2009—when my vision recovered and I was truly "seeing" my life for the first time in years—I quit my comfy corporate job as a global marketer to become "a free-spirited but fiercely focused mistress of my own destiny." That's what I wrote down on a Post-it note my first day of self-employment. But, uh—what did that really mean? How I was going to, you know, make *money*?

Corporate Gina used to sneak out of bed at 2 A.M. to write, read, and explore. I felt I had to do that "fun" part of my life in the off-hours. But I was tired of silencing my creative curiosities, quenching them only in the dark of night. I knew I had to bring my creative spirit and my passions into the light of day. What I soon learned was that there are a lot of people like me out there: people who are not satisfied to leave a huge part of their personalities behind every day when they leave for the office. People who want to find a way to be happier in their work and their lives. I decided I could help them.

My passion was to spend my days teaching, writing, and motivating others to unleash their genius. Since I had spent fifteen years of my professional life helping companies market and brand products, I thought, "Well, if I can help companies brand and launch products successfully—why can't I help launch *people*?"

The human mash-up of my "softer" qualitative assets (the community organizer, leadership development trainer, and inspirational catalyst—the more emotional and passionate side of myself), combined with my "harder" quantitative assets (the sharp, strategic, highly skilled corporate Gina who had succeeded in the business world for more than a decade), resulted in something new: a coaching and training practice that would empower people to discover and market their own distinctive assets. (More on "soft assets" and "hard assets" in the next chapter.)

It was a great idea, I thought, and with my business plan in hand, I was ready to find clients and launch my new career. The world, though, just wasn't cooperating at first. The *nerve* of the universe to launch into a full-on economic crisis just as I was having my epiphany!

Still, with great excitement (and, I'll confess, a small loan from my mom), I set out to launch my new company—Genuine Insights, named for the moment of my own epiphany. With the recession now in full thorny bloom, I lit out on my yellow brick road, intending to pull every motivated seeker I could find into the journey with me.

They say that a recession is a great time to start a new venture, and I have to say that in my experience it's true. It's a fertile time for risk and exploration. Somehow, for all of the desperation in the air, there is also a great deal of creative impulse and a unique sense of promise. I actually didn't have any trouble finding clients who were ready for the life-changing transformation I knew I could help them achieve. Finding them was the easy part.

But shortly after I began working with them, I realized the sad truth: that most of my clients had absolutely no idea who they were or what they stood for. They had come to me because they knew they were missing something, but they didn't know what it was. How could I help people build brands around their human assets if they had no idea who they really were?

That's when I realized that "it" was the unique selling proposition for each of us—the place where all our contradictions converge, the precise spot where the hard and the soft assets we all possess meet and reveal the wide world of potential in each of us.

Initially focusing on branding and marketing my clients' unique points of differentiation was putting the cart before the horse. I had to go back to the drawing board and identify what my "horse" actually was—it was helping people, teams, and organizations identify and cultivate *genius*, which was the unrealized asset so clearly missing for all of them. The marketing and branding—the "cart"—could come only when this singular asset had been identified, cultivated, and set in motion. Once I understood that the crux of my work was identifying and unleashing their genius, everything began to click. So what was an astonishing personal discovery for myself became the basis of a brand-new approach for professionals who were just as ready as I had been to realize their true potential.

Here's how I know I've found my "it": Since the start of my business in 2009, when I launched the "practical genius" concept into the world, I have been traveling around the globe, working with organizations and individuals on where to find practical genius, how to master it, and what to do with it to transform their lives. The ability to recognize a need, change directions, and start a movement around the importance of modern genius was *my* moment of genius. This book will show you how to find *your* genius and share it with the world.

Practical Genius is about going to the edges of who you are and making it happen for yourself—and not waiting for illness, disease, or temporary blindness to do it. It's about owning your destiny—which for me is akin to constantly hearing a symphony of my passions in my head. It is a buffet, every day, of all your favorite foods. Owning your own destiny and waking up to do what your heart, mind, and soul were intended to do is liberation. For me, that is the end—and the beginning. It is the Promised Land. It is freedom.

Do not be mistaken, however. Finding your personal genius is no small task. Identifying and realizing your own dreams will be hard work. It is risky and sometimes painful, in the way a really difficult, intense workout can be. But it's also good, it's healthy, and it's based on pure passion.

So many of us compromise our passions for our strengths and end up working at what we do best rather than what we love to do. It doesn't have to be that way! *Practical Genius* is about intertwining your strengths, your passions, and your values to establish the complete, original formula for *your* success. All too often, it is only when we are faced with the fragility of life that we realize that wasting twelve hours a day doing something we don't love doing is a mistake. In reality, it shouldn't take something radical or revolutionary happening to force us to stop letting life de-genius us.

If you're one of the people who think you don't really have a choice and simply "have to do what you have to do" to survive or support your family, this book is for you. You *do* have a choice. You just haven't stepped up with your practical genius because of fear or because you've been conditioned to believe that there are certain choices that are simply not available to you.

I'm not just going to shower you with platitudes. In *Practical Genius,* I'm going to show you how to do it.

The first step: you must take inventory of your strengths and passions and analyze your current reality. Are you living your most authentic purposeful life, or is there something missing? I work on changing the lives of my clients every day, and when I get them to push beyond their comfort zones and to commit to their innate genius a little each day, it's always amazing to hear how, over time, step by step, they change and the circumstances around them change for the better.

TEST YOUR GENIUS

Let's start by taking a little snapshot of who you are and where you are right now. This diagnostic will help you measure some common challenges and opportunities before we begin your journey to genius. One of my mentors, Sheila Wellington, used to say, "Gina, we treasure what we measure," and I have learned over time how true that really is. So, before you begin your genius journey, let's benchmark how close or how far you are from living a practical genius life right now. This five-minute test will be a wake-up call for you and should be viewed as your very own personal genius starting block.

Directions: For each item below, circle the number that most closely describes how you view yourself today. Then add up all of your answers and compare your total to the interpretation key at the end of the test.
1 = The statement on the left best describes me
10 = The statement on the right best describes me

My values are often superseded by the values of others in my professional and personal life.	1 2 3 4 5 6 7 8 9 10	I am a value-driven individual; I never compromise my values under any circumstances.
I am motivated by extrinsic (material) values rather than by intrinsic (internal) values.	1 2 3 4 5 6 7 8 9 10	I am motivated by intrinsic (internal) values rather than by extrinsic (material) values.
The values of the organization I work for are very different from my personal values.	1 2 3 4 5 6 7 8 9 10	My values are 100% aligned with the values of the organization I work for.
I used to know what my passions are, but today I am not sure.	1 2 3 4 5 6 7 8 9 10	I know exactly what my passions are and honor them daily.
My passions are not a priority in my life; I nurture them only when time permits.	1 2 3 4 5 6 7 8 9 10	My passions are a priority in my life, and I invest time and resources in them.

I do not participate in activities at work or at home that nurture my passions.	1 2 3 4 5 6 7 8 9 10	I am able to engage in my passions both at home and at work.
I exercise my creative abilities at home more than at work.	1 2 3 4 5 6 7 8 9 10	I incorporate my creative abilities into all aspects of my life, as much at work as at home
I am not sure what my creative talents are.	1 2 3 4 5 6 7 8 9 10	I know and exercise my creative talents daily both at work and outside of work.
I do not think creativity matters in my personal life or in my work.	1 2 3 4 5 6 7 8 9 10	Creativity is something I value and nurture both in my personal life and in my work.
I use the left (logical) side of my brain more than the right (creative) side.	1 2 3 4 5 6 7 8 9 10	I use my whole mind regularly, and one side doesn't dominate the other.
I do not seek extraordinary, personal growth-oriented experiences.	1 2 3 4 5 6 7 8 9 10	Realizing my ultimate personal potential is a constant priority for me.
I consider myself a novice and rookie in my industry and market sector.	1 2 3 4 5 6 7 8 9 10	I consider myself an expert in my industry and market sector.
I have never been rewarded or recognized for my expertise.	1 2 3 4 5 6 7 8 9 10	I have been rewarded and recognized at least once for my expertise.
Although I am an expert in my field, I do not leverage my expertise outside the requirements of my job.	1 2 3 4 5 6 7 8 9 10	I market myself as an expert in my field beyond the requirements of my job.
My strengths are not being fully utilized.	1 2 3 4 5 6 7 8 9 10	Strategic application of my strengths adds greatly to my productivity.
I cannot articulate what my three greatest strengths are.	1 2 3 4 5 6 7 8 9 10	I have clear understanding of what my three greatest strengths are, and I utilize this knowledge to push myself forward and excel.

I am not able to leverage my strengths at work on a regular basis.	1 2 3 4 5 6 7 8 9 10	I leverage my strengths at work every day.
My skill set has gone unchanged in the last ten years.	1 2 3 4 5 6 7 8 9 10	I am regularly expanding and enhancing my skill set.
My professional development is more important to me than my personal development.	1 2 3 4 5 6 7 8 9 10	My personal development is more important to me than my professional development.
I work in my current role and occupation because I have to, not because I want to.	1 2 3 4 5 6 7 8 9 10	I enjoy my work and feel rewarded for my efforts and accomplishments both financially and emotionally.

Interpretation of Practical Genius Factor:

0–44: Coma. You are far from living a life of practical genius. Immediate action is required.

45–69: Serious. Fear is a major dynamic, and you avoid expressing your genius, which is a formidable obstacle to your growth and well-being.

70–94: Stifled. You feel helpless and stuck. Your talent and energy are not in play.

95–119: Barely tolerable. You are showing up for life but are apathetic both intellectually and emotionally.

120–144: Comfortable. You are creative and things get done, but there is little "spark" to take things to the next level.

145–169: Satisfactory. You are striving toward performance, and occasional strokes of genius appear.

170–194: Great. You are engaged, energetic, and innovative. This is fertile ground for exceptional results.

195–200: Excellent. Practical genius is in the house!

THE ANATOMY OF A PRACTICAL GENIUS

Practical genius is your jillion-dollar personal portfolio of brilliance. It's the secret code within you that only you can crack. But once you do, the possibilities are endless.

Contrary to the traditional beliefs about genius, practical genius is based on the truth that each of us possesses genius deep inside and it's just waiting to be activated and set in motion. That's what practical genius is all about: identifying and leveraging both the soft and hard unique personal assets each of us possesses. Of course, it's also about using those assets to open doors, attract opportunity, leverage personal power, and succeed beyond your wildest dreams.

Here's how it works:

Identify your genius. This means consciously acknowledging and taking active responsibility for your unique strengths, skills, expertise, passions, creativity, and values. Hint: the intersection of these quantitative and qualitative characteristics is where your practical genius lies. It requires a particular kind of self-assessment, a series of reflective exercises that enable you to identify the genius ingredients that you possess. This extraction phase of work represents your very own genius full-body scan. I promise it won't hurt.

Express your genius. The greatest challenge for most people—which is rarely addressed in leadership models—is visibility. If you are not actively, purposefully sharing your unique narrative with the world, you're compromising your personal and professional impact. This chapter is all about your story and how you share it. Think of this as a long-overdue opportunity to tell the *real* story.

Expressing your genius is about turning that sweet spot where your hard and soft assets meet into the story you tell others. A person without a story is invisible. It's here that I will ask you to consider a range of aspects of your expression, including your narrative, your themes, your vocabulary, and your visuals. Expressing genius is about not leaving any side of yourself out of the game. It all matters. Enough with the same narratives; here we will push the bar and begin to tell new provocative, daring, inspiring stories about who you are and why you matter.

Surround yourself with genius. You are who you walk with. Raise the bar, and build your network with others who are living purposeful, inspired lives. This is about reaching out in a nontransactional way and cultivating meaningful, deeply valuable relationships. Raise your expectations, elevate your standards, and surround yourself with people who are a positive reflection of your genius.

We have many kinds of relationships in our lives, and who we spend our time with is critical to improving and building upon our goals and experiences. This chapter will introduce you to the kinds of relationships we should be cultivating every day—our Yodas (mentors), our ambassadors (cheerleaders), our "fat brains" (smart young people), and a tribe (our crew). Once you have identified who is on your wish list for each of these types of relationships, I will walk you through a simple process that has opened many a door in my own life. These are the rules of engagement and a blueprint for building the genius relationships you want to have.

Sustain your genius. Living your practical genius requires rededicating yourself to its mastery every day. This means cultivating a constant focus on committing to a practice that naturally suits your genius. And as with any successful behavioral model, it requires applying measurements and personal accountability. Broken down into practical terms, this chapter offers you new daily routines that will keep you healthy, productive, and prosperous. It's one thing to decide to reach for greatness, something else entirely to sustain it. What it boils down to is resilience, staying focused on growth, and holding yourself accountable to your own genius. This means making the right choices for your body and mind, keeping your professional and personal lives deeply connected in order to reap and enjoy the benefits of a life lived within a genius zone.

This chapter is the most important; without constant sustenance, we fall back upon bad habits. Sustaining genius involves a range of factors, from incorporating brain food into your diet to exercises that work your creative muscles to establishing rituals that stimulate your intuition. You'll even create a mantra to help hold you accountable to your daily genius life. Sustaining real smarts takes discipline and commitment. I never said it would be easy.

Market your genius. This is where the game really changes. When you project and broadcast your genius consistently, with clear purpose and passion, your personal and professional dynamic shifts into crazy growth mode. This chapter is dedicated to leveraging what is distinct and original about your genius to attract, engage, and grow your natural audience. When you are living and working at the intersection of all your assets, you're marketing your genius on all frequencies.

It's rare that someone can promise you that what they are going to teach you will make you a better person. But that is what I am promising you. I am turning on all the lights, opening the doors and windows, and clearing out the closets to set you on the path to the transformation of your life. When I decided to live my practical genius, I remember feeling guilty about how much fun I was having. "Work is never fun, Gina. There's probably something wrong with this," I told myself. This was just the de-genius devil on my shoulder, trying to throw me off my destiny. Instead of internalizing these false ideas, I learned to shut them up and embrace a more natural, exciting, and truly pleasurable approach toward life. My mother used to say, "Everything that is natural is good for you." Working from a place of obligation and routine for a paycheck is not natural. Working for joy, innovation, and autonomy is.

That's it for the practical genius foreplay. It's time to get your genius on.

IDENTIFY YOUR GENIUS

Only You Can Find It

START WITH THE HEART IN MIND

When I coach my clients on identifying their practical genius and why it matters, the first question I present to them—what I like to refer to as the billion-dollar question—may be the most important one in this entire book:

> When you are long gone from this world, what is the legacy you would have liked to leave behind?

This is the kind of loaded question that makes people nervous. But I promise that if you make yourself think about it, you will begin to have a visceral image of what you really care about and what you would like your life to have represented.

The idea is to be the master designer of your legacy and to think of your legacy as what's in your heart—what you really love—right alongside what your mind is capable of accomplishing. Learn from the legacy of Alfred Nobel, who is best known for creating the Nobel Peace Prize. In fact, his most significant accomplishments during his lifetime were his invention of dynamite, explosives, and other inventions useful to the art of making war. At the time of his death he controlled factories for the manufacture of explosives in many parts of the world, but he was smart enough to ensure that his legacy was his greatest passion, which was world peace. Before he died, he set aside $9 million to set up a fund to establish yearly prizes for merit in physics, chemistry, medicine or physiology, literature, and world peace— the honor we know today as the Nobel Peace Prize. A true practical genius, Alfred Nobel made his wealth from his inventive mind but left his legacy from the heart.

If your legacy image is filled with accomplishments (degrees from fancy schools, social or corporate status, possessions, or wealth, for example), close your eyes and try to imagine it again—this time coming from a place of passion, not accomplishment. What do you see? Is it a meaningful project you led? Is it something you created with your own initiative? Maybe it's a dynamic relationship you were a part of. If this is the kind of thing you see, now you're getting somewhere!

But if you really can't conjure up even a picture of your legacy—if you haven't had a BlackBerry-free minute even to contemplate tomorrow because you are barely surviving and managing today—you need this chapter more than ever. In fact, you can't afford *not* to take a moment to ruminate on this question.

I have always believed in the power of starting with the end in mind. If you take the time and effort to visualize the destiny you truly desire from a perspective of passion and accomplishment, you set yourself up to establish goals, create agendas, and seek opportunities that will push you closer to your legacy, which you will discover is a true product of your ambitious self and your conscious self. Having goals simply for the sake of having goals sends you on a fruitless, uninspiring life's journey. Having goals that point you toward the legacy you want to realize makes the journey rewarding and real.

YOUR "OTHER G-SPOT"

Now that you have allowed yourself a glimpse of your life's purpose, let's talk about how it relates to where your genius really lives. If genius were to have a physical address, it would be located somewhere between your heart and your mind. Specifically, it lives at the intersection of what I call your hard assets (your skills, strengths, and expertise—the quantitative talents you've developed, usually on the job) and your soft assets (your passions, creativity, and values—the qualitative talents that are tougher to quantify but no less important). I like to refer to this intersection as "the other G-spot."

Passions Values Creative Ability
Soft Personal Assets

G
{The "Sweet" Spot}

Practical
Genius
Model

Hard Professional Assets
Skills | Strengths | Expertise

It's rare to accidentally stumble on the place where your heart and mind click. So rather than hoping to get lucky, I'm going to help you get to the other G-spot, which is where the truth and essence of your practical genius resides. When you identify the spot where your soft and hard assets intersect, the process of realizing your personal power begins.

This affects you in a personally profound way that catapults you forward in your professional experience. As you grow and your genius develops, your skill in closing deals, negotiating, and navigating important professional relationships will become more confident, more effective, more precise. Your genius will become your currency on every level, and its impact on your success in business (whether you are a corporate executive or an entrepreneur) will be nothing short of amazing.

To get an idea of what life looks like in this genius zone, consider your life an absolute acceptance of contradiction, where there isn't a battle between the personal you and the professional you any longer. The life of practical genius is one life, a healthy marriage between your heart (what you care most about) and your mind (the manifestation of your intellectual curiosities, strengths, and expertise). Think of your other G-spot as the ultimate measure by which you make every decision, whether it's choosing your next employer, your next lover, or the next place you want to live. You can also consider it a formula that will never fail to hold you accountable to staying at the authentic, powerful core of who you are.

The other G-spot is a place that is never tilted too far toward the soft (personal) side of who you are nor too far toward the hard (professional) side of who you are. Think of the little bubble of air in a carpenter's level. When the bubble is squarely in the middle of the viewer, there is perfect balance. In *you,* that bubble is your other G-spot. Once you find it and learn to stay there, life becomes much easier, goals become more attainable, relationships prosper, and you will find that achieving results is far easier.

Ultimately, as you get comfortable residing in your other G-spot, you will begin to notice which environments are most conducive for you, which relationships support your genius, and which activities allow both sides of you to engage harmoniously—and dynamically. With practice, your entire life will be kicked up a notch just by your having a constant measure of the ideal intersection of your heart and mind.

In my own life, I use my other G-spot as my benchmark for every decision I make, from the foods I choose to eat to how I spend my time, even to how I facilitate meetings. For example, when I meet with prospects, I strategically open up the meetings with soft-asset probing questions about interests, inner passions, and desires, exploring the sweeter soft side of their lives. Once they are a little "emotionally undressed," I nudge them toward the business discussion, always managing the flow of the conversation so that it never veers too far toward the mind nor too far toward the heart. They don't know it, but I'm keeping the meeting within their practical genius zone as well as my own. The result is always powerful; 75 percent of the time the outcome is new business, and 99 percent of the time it's a new, meaningful relationship. Many are wowed by our "first date" together, and what's fascinating is that the "wow" has nothing to do with me and everything to do with my ability to keep their other G-spot stimulated. It's extremely effective to frame your experiences—both small and large—within the genius zone.

Whether managing a career change, a new relationship, or a routine sales call, your experiences are transformed from everyday to extraordinary.

The big secret to implementing this model and to unleashing possibilities you may not even know exist within yourself is maintaining and working on all assets simultaneously, without favoring one area over another. Everyone has a different G-spot, and once you know where yours is, you can really see what's possible when you stimulate it in others.

In order to get to that spot, however, we first have to identify and extract the six basic ingredients of your genius. On the hard asset side, there are skills, strengths, and expertise; on the soft asset side, there are passions, creative abilities, and values.

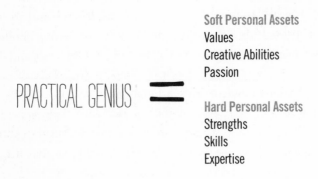

PRACTICAL GENIUS **=**

Soft Personal Assets
Values
Creative Abilities
Passion

Hard Personal Assets
Strengths
Skills
Expertise

FIRST IDENTIFY YOUR HARD ASSETS

What exactly are hard assets? Your hard assets are the concrete attributes that make up the professional you and are the foundation and framework of your practical genius. They are a critical component of your overall human capital. I use the vocabulary usually associated with one's financial portfolio on purpose. If you try to examine yourself through some sort of soft-focus lens, you'll never really grasp or appreciate what's at stake.

The simplest way to view your hard assets is to think of your skills, strengths, and expertise. These are the professional capabilities that are predominantly cultivated on the left (logical) side of your brain. You have likely been programmed to assess your market value based on those attributes since you were a child. Hard assets are the skills, strengths, and areas of expertise that are highlighted and glorified on your résumé and that for most people are the best measure of human capital, at least in the workplace. That's because those are the assets that are measurable within a common context of accomplishment. As we move closer to your other G-spot, you'll see that this is only part of the asset side of your balance sheet.

Your hard assets include all of your natural and cultivated aptitudes and skills. They are what landed you your first job and are what you are most often measured by today. What is interesting about our hard assets is how so many of us have framed our adult lives and identities around these predominantly professional, work-related qualities. For example, if you are a doctor, your life is defined by the role that encompasses the aptitudes and skills required to be a doctor. If you are an economist, your identity is structured around that expertise. We have become our titles, and our titles have become us. But in truth, they are very limited descriptors of our hard assets.

Skills

Now, for you to begin to decipher which are your leading hard assets, let's begin to look at each area, beginning with skills. Skills are the functional abilities we use every day on the job and are basically what we've practiced over the years and come to do well. Consider your skills what you went to school to learn as well as what you have honed and sharpened (and been compensated for) over the course of your professional life. You weren't born with your current skill set; you have spent most of your professional life working on your skills, and they are an obvious contributor to your bottom line.

The marketing guru Seth Godin once blogged that skills are either your domain knowledge or your process knowledge. Domain knowledge, for example, would be something like "playing the piano" or "writing copy about furniture." Process knowledge refers to the "emotional intelligence skills you have about managing projects, visualizing success, persuading other people of your point of view or dealing with multiple priorities."

When you think of your skills, are they predominately made up of domain knowledge or process knowledge related to emotional intelligence? Today emotional intelligence matters more than anything and can include people skills, leadership skills, communication skills, problem-solving skills, and analytical skills. Let's look at each of these top five skills.

People Skills

Many people argue that today, "people skills" are the most important skills one can possess. They include the ability to relate to, inspire, and mitigate conflict with your employees, coworkers, customers, and partners. These interpersonal skills basically reflect an aptitude for building and maintaining valuable relationships.

I have a friend who is renowned for her people skills. The people she works with call her "the glue" because she has such a knack for doing what's necessary to make workplace relationships an asset, not a drag on the organization. Lots of people believe they have good people skills—"Sure, people like me!" they think. But when it comes down to it, there's much more to it than likability. When you think of yourself in relation to others, do you see yourself as a good people reader, a fixer, or a facilitator? Or are you one of the ones who is brought along by the person with the people skills?

Leadership Skills

Though there is debate about whether leadership is an ability people are born with or is cultivated, these skills deal with your ability to manage teams to accomplish goals and to inspire initiative in others. Leadership skills also involve your ability to maintain a productive climate and to motivate, mobilize, and meet high performance standards.

When you read the word "leadership," do you think of yourself as a leader, or do you immediately think of someone else? Some people demur from thinking of themselves as leaders, seeing the word "leadership" as intimidating, cold, and arrogantly individualistic, when in fact it is a critically important function in any society. A leader has the capacity and confidence to draw others toward a desired conclusion. This quality has saved the day countless times through history and plays a crucial, often memorable role in human events. If you come by it naturally or it's been cultivated in you over a lifetime, you know it. You're the one saying "Let's do it this way." And the others do.

Communication Skills

Communication skills are commonly considered to be the ability to listen, write, and speak effectively. I would further suggest that these skills include the ability to conceptualize and articulate concepts in a way that enables others to actualize them. The act of communicating involves verbal, nonverbal, and paraverbal components. The verbal component refers to the content of your message. The nonverbal component refers to the message you send through your body language. And the paraverbal component refers to how you use your voice and tone in conveying messages.

Do you have a clear sense of how—and how well—you communicate with others? Does it come easily or naturally to you, or have you developed a confidence in your communications competence? Alternatively, are you happier to count on others to lead presentations, write reports, tell stories, explain the truth?

Whether you think of yourself as a have or a have-not when it comes to communication, it's important to note that tapping your practical genius requires that you use those muscles. Don't say I didn't warn you.

Problem-Solving Skills

Problem-solving skills include the ability to find solutions to problems using your reasoning and past experience along with available information and resources. This skill is demonstrated by a strong facility for generating workable solutions where others cannot. People who are strong problem solvers are usually adaptable, tend to be able to visualize a problem and solution beforehand, and are great at creating "workarounds."

Do you have the ability to see the warning signs for a problem, resulting in proactive attempts to avoid the problem or to adapt the approach? Do people tend to come to you to help them "figure stuff out"? Do people usually want you on their team because you're such a productive player? Or do you find yourself more often doing the leg-work of solving a problem rather than innovating the solution? This is one of the skills that's easiest to map on one of those aptitude tests they used to give you as a kid.

Analytical Skills

Analytical skills deal with your ability to assess a situation, seek mul-tiple perspectives, gather and process more information if necessary, and identify key issues that need to be addressed and resolved. The ability to identify, scrutinize, and streamline complex work processes is a function of this skill. The person with analytical skills sits some-where between the leader and the problem solver in terms of the prac-tical applicability of his or her skills on a project or in an organization.

If you have the strong ability to apply logical thinking to gathering and processing information, designing and testing solutions to prob-lems, and formulating plans, you're the analytical type. You are often asked to lead teams because of your ability to decipher, prioritize, and address challenges in order to meet the objective.

To me, these five skills (people, leadership, communication, problem solving, and analytical) are the most comprehensive, highest-level skills one can possess. Of course there are many others, often more specific but also often related to the five high-level skills. But thinking about your skills in these terms will help give shape to these assets in your mind.

PLAYBOOK

Sketch Your Skill Set

Have a look at the list below and see if any sound familiar to you—and *about* you. Try to tick off your high-level skills (in bold below) and/or your ten top more specific skills.

___ Administrative support

___ Administering programs

___ Advising people

___ **Analytical skills**

___ Assembling components

___ Attention to detail

___ Auditing

___ Bringing people together

___ Budgeting

___ Calculating

___ Checking for accuracy

___ Coaching people

___ **Communication skills**

___ Compiling data

___ Creating ideas

___ Customer service

___ Decision making

___ Delegation

___ Drawing plans and
diagrams

___ Editing

___ Enforcing rules and policy

___ Evaluating performance

___ Financial management

___ Fundraising

___ Generating new
business

___ Handling complaints

___ Interpreting information

___ Interpreting language

___ Inventing concepts

___ Implementing new policy
and procedures

___ **Leadership skills**

___ Listening

___ Managing people

___ Manipulating numbers

___ Meeting deadlines

___ Motivating people

___ Negotiating

___ Organizing

___ **People skills**

___ Performing
demonstrations or
presentations

___ Persuading people

___ Planning meetings/events
___ **Problem-solving skills**
___ Promoting products or
     services
___ Public speaking
___ Reaching conclusions
     based on research
___ Recognizing problems
___ Relating to people
___ Research
___ Selling

___ Setting goals
___ Setting standards
___ Sorting data
___ Teamwork
___ Technology
___ Troubleshooting
___ Visualization
___ Working with regulations
___ Working with your hands
___ Writing

This list is by no means exhaustive, but it does get you thinking about the tools in your toolbox. By now you must have realized that great teams and organizations include members who together possess a whole range of these various necessary skills. Think of Mark Zuckerberg, his cofounders of Facebook, and the amazing team he now has to propel the company forward at the speed of light. That company represents the mother lode of skill sets—and I guarantee that a key handful of practical geniuses are among them!

Strengths

Your strengths are the second major component of your hard assets. The path to excellence lies in our strengths, yet most people haven't a clue what their strengths are. As the leadership expert Peter Drucker noted, "When asked to define their strengths, people often reply with skills or knowledge—the wrong answer. All great leadership begins with a deep understanding of one's strengths and the strengths of those around them."

According to the Gallup Organization Consultant and author Tom Rath, "Talent, described as your natural way of thinking, feeling or behaving multiplied by investment, the time spent practicing, developing your skills and building your knowledge base is what defines a person's strengths, ultimately defined as the ability to consistently provide near-perfect performance."

I tend to think of strengths as mostly adjectives, while skills tend to be nouns. This isn't always true, but it's a helpful way to think about them. Some of the strengths you might discover you have include:

- **Deliberative,** which exemplifies those who identify, manage, and ultimately try to reduce risk.
- **Futuristic,** a strength that is just what you'd think. You daydream about the future, imagine what could be, and are able to express a vision of the future that excites you and those around you.
- **Strategic,** a skill that can't be taught, a way of thinking that recognizes patterns where others see chaos. You are a chess player who can imagine the next six moves.

To begin to think about your strengths, take a moment to reflect on your past performance evaluations or 360-degree reviews. These traditional assessments typically measure what you're good at and identify areas where you're lacking. Think of the skills, abilities, and performance traits that most often are identified as strengths in these meetings. Make a short list of tasks and project areas in which you excel and basically hit it out of the park every time. Try to identify not just the tool (the skill) that enables you to do well but also the aspects of your nature that contribute to your success.

If you're a free agent or work for an organization that doesn't provide a constructive review process, just answer this simple question: What do you do best? Generate a list that encompasses your professional and personal experience, the projects you participate in at work or in your community, even talents that contribute to the success of your home life. For example, do colleagues seek you out for their projects because you're a creative problem solver? Are you the one who keeps your family on track, thinking ten steps ahead for each of you? Are you recognized as someone who can champion an idea, build consensus on a team, or take a project all the way to the finish line? The qualities that enable your skills and capacities are your defining strengths.

Here's a way to think about your strengths:

What activities do you actually love doing because you enjoy doing them well? Do you look forward to doing them whenever possible?

What do you do well and effortlessly? What is it about your nature or personality that enables your success in this area?

Say you're an Olympic swimmer. Besides excellent technique, physical strength, and lots and lots of training, what contributes to your success in this sport? Your competitive nature, your discipline, your precision, and your perseverance, for starters.

When you look at what you do well and can identify the underlying reasons for your success, you're looking at your strengths.

Expertise

Now that you've considered your skills and strengths, take a moment to consider your expertise, the most important of all hard assets. Your expertise is the body of knowledge over which you have the most mastery and authority. It's the area of your professional life you have most invested in and was probably the focus of most of your education and training. Whatever your expertise—whether it be social media, specialty food, medical devices, or fitness training—it is probably the thing that has the greatest value within your portfolio of hard assets.

When I work with individual clients and ask them what their expertise is, some will say, "Well, I don't know if I can call myself an expert, but I've spent the last fifteen years working on (fill in the blank)." Hello! You've spent fifteen years studying, working, and building capability within one subject area? That definitely makes you an expert, kiddo!

So if you are hesitating when considering your own expertise, remember that an expert is any individual who exhibits the highest level of mastery and performance of a specialized job, task, or skill. Since there isn't an expert fairy who drops in to grant you the "expert" title, I will. Whatever your primary subject matter, from here forward think of yourself as an expert in that area. This isn't to say you know all there is to know about it or don't have infinite room to increase your experience and knowledge in that area. It's really just to say you're more of an expert than you might think you are. In fact, you're more of an expert than most!

For example, one of my clients is a professional skydiver and instructor with more than twenty years of skydiving and ten thousand jumps under his belt. He recently realized during a full day of our working together that his expertise isn't just the act of skydiving; more important, he is an expert in what he calls the "extreme focus" that is required to succeed as a skydiver. Using the same techniques he has used for sixteen years teaching people to skydive, he is now teaching others how to have a laser-beam, lifesaving kind of focus in other areas of their lives. He has leveraged his core strength and has further identified and refined his expertise.

If you have to pull out your résumé to help you identify your hard assets, do it! The goal of this first step is to get you to visualize the professional ingredients that contribute to the foundation of your practical genius.

Once you've assessed the ingredients that make up the professional you—the hard you, the logical you—you are ready to begin the exploration of the soft assets that contribute to the spice, zest, and energy of your genius. Although your hard professional assets may seem at odds with your soft personal assets, they are actually highly interconnected and interdependent. So move through the following ideas with an open mind and be prepared to discover the rest of the ingredients that give rise and reality to your genius.

NOW IDENTIFY YOUR SOFT ASSETS

So many of us check half of our identities at the door when we enter our workplace each day. We leverage only our hard assets, and then we wonder why we feel disconnected when reflecting on our personal lives versus our professional lives. The qualities we usually ascribe to our personal lives and our private selves are what I call our soft assets—simply defined as our passions, creativity, and values.

Think about folks you know who've been on a track for twenty-plus years and complain of feeling dissatisfied and stuck. You'd feel miserable, too, if you were constantly striving to succeed with one hand tied behind your back, without the benefit of some of the most powerful and effective qualities you possess. We focus on our hard assets and undervalue and sublimate our soft assets—what a waste of half of who we are! The greatest lesson I've learned is that in order to become the person you really want to be, you have to flip that paradigm.

Today's workforce needs professionals who can think inside, outside, and all around the box. We need professionals with empathy who can design collaborative initiatives from the heart to fight longstanding, intractable problems. Today people need to honor their innate desire to be autonomous and not have to sit in gray boxes for eight hours a day with carrots in front of them to get them to perform. The way we work is changing, which means we will not be alone in shifting the way we express ourselves and the way we go about integrating our work, play, and passions. The first step in making this paradigm shift is to know exactly what your soft personal assets are—and to put them in the proper place on your balance sheet.

What are your soft assets? They are the innate qualities of the heart you possess and probably lead with on the weekends! Soft assets are the best parts of the personal you, the one who dances on Saturday nights, jogs on Sunday mornings, and plays hopscotch with your kid in the driveway while waiting for the school bus. You've identified your hard assets; now let's look at what makes up your soft assets—your passions, creativity, and values.

Passions

Take a moment to think about your passions. What would you be doing every day if money weren't an issue? How would you spend your time and other personal resources if you had infinite freedom and no restraints? Some passions have long been known as hobbies or favorite activities, but they're really more than that. Your passions are where your mind wanders when you're in a meeting that's gone on too long or you're waiting to catch a plane or riding the subway to work. Whether it's cooking, playing the bassoon, or doing tae kwon do, in the end the passions we pursue contain major ingredients of our practical genius.

What if you've ignored your passions and interests for so long that when asked you really can't think of any? Don't panic. Close your eyes for a moment and think about what they were when you were sixteen. Summon your sense memories to remind you of what those passions looked like, tasted like, and sounded like, and how they made you feel. Once you have a visual, hold on to it and consider it the foundation for the passion part of your genius development.

For many of us, our form of play is our greatest passion, so don't ignore play when considering your passion. Kevin Carroll, the renowned leader of the play movement, believes we all can find our inner genius through play: "Once you find your source of play let it be your life's work so much so that no one, not even you, will be able to tell the difference between work and play."

Use the notion of play as a prompt to think about your passions:

If you had twenty-four hours left to live, how would you spend your play time? (NB: You are not allowed to say "with family"!)

If I were your fairy godmother and could wave a wand and transport you to your happiest, most joyful place, where would that be? And what would you be doing there?

We all have a "hard-on" for something. Come on, you know you do. What is it? Is it food, dance, travel, reading, adventure sports, fishing, golf, music, technology, fitness?

One last tip for identifying your passions: think of one word that captures the be-all and end-all for you. I call this your "ultimate word." My ultimate word is "freedom," and each of my passions—traveling, scuba diving, and writing—gives me a euphoric feeling of freedom. What is the ultimate word for you? What does it say about your passions?

Creativity

When was the last time you really used your creativity? Do you even think of yourself as a creative person? Or are you a "card-carrying" creative person who uses her creative abilities daily? Think about it: when was the last time you painted, sang a song, wrote a poem, came up with a new idea, or built something? Creativity is all those things and more; it's your ability to make new connections between existing ideas or concepts. What is most interesting is that it's fueled by the process of either conscious or unconscious insight. Whether you use it rarely or every day, you need to take a moment and think about your capacity for creativity. And think hard about it, because today it matters perhaps more than any other quantifiable human asset.

In fact, creativity represents the new competitive advantage in corporate America. Why? Because it is only through creativity that we can begin to solve problems, innovate, and create better lives for our communities and ourselves. Organizations are seeking out MFAs at a faster rate than MBAs. And employers are beginning to recognize that creative talent is actually good for business during a recession, and some are beginning to give their employees opportunities to explore many realms of expression in the regular course of their work.

Problem solving and reasoning are directly connected to creativity. Oprah Winfrey's dear friend and life coach Martha Beck once told me, "Gina, the foundation of all genius is always looking for the problems because they open the doors to solutions." She's right. Engaging your creativity, reasoning, and past experiences will lead you to solutions that are expressions of your practical genius.

Now, if you are experiencing a bit of resistance to assessing your creativity, understand that it's your inner critic speaking and it's time to learn to manage her well. When considering the fear you may be experiencing in acknowledging your creativity, consider this quote from one of my favorite books, *The War of Art* by Steven Pressfield: "Most of us have two lives. The life we live, and the unlived life within us. Between the two stands Resistance." Your inner critic is resistance, and the resistance within each of us acts as a hindrance to our creative potential. "Creative work is not a selfish act or a bid for attention on the part of the actor," Pressfield wrote. "It's a gift to the world and every being in it. Don't cheat us of your contribution. Give us what you've got."

So what is it you've got? To give it credence and specificity in your own mind, take some time to think back over your whole life, even to your earliest childhood. What experiences do you remember giving you the unique satisfaction of having made or expressed something that didn't exist before you did it? It doesn't have to be something you held in your hand—it can be an idea, a phrase of music, a compelling combination of plants in your garden, even an outfit you wore once. It just needs to have been an original expression of something original about you.

If you're not already in touch with your creative side, this may take a while to mull over. Search hard through the nooks and crannies of your experience, shake the moments and memories out of the trees of your life. Eventually (I promise!) you will end up with a small collection of sometimes similar, sometimes disparate glistenings that represent the components of your creativity. Write a short but detailed description of each of those creative moments you shook from your tree. They don't make you Picasso, but they do prove once and for all that creativity lives in each of us. Many of us chose to bury it long ago, preferring to watch and admire "creative people" from the sidelines of our own lives. Practical genius does not allow this; creativity is not a spectator sport.

Values

A value is a belief, mission, or philosophy that is meaningful; it can range from the concrete, such as a belief in hard work and punctuality, to the more abstract, such as self-reliance, forthrightness, and authenticity.

Whether we are consciously aware of them or not, each of us has a core set of personal values, and these values are what motivates our genius. The problem for a lot of people is that they have trouble articulating their values. The late, great journalist Edward R. Murrow had a radio show called *This I Believe.* Each week he featured an essay written by notables of the time, such as President Harry Truman or the dancer Martha Graham, as well as by ordinary folks like you and me. The essays strove to express what the essayists believed in, what core values or day-to-day truths helped them live true lives. The pieces were, as you can imagine, surprising, touching, and, above all, deeply personal.

Ask the next person you see, even someone you know well, "Hey, what do you believe in?" You'll be shocked at how many good, accomplished, highly principled people will have trouble answering the question.

More than any other aspect of your makeup, your values are the closest, most accurate reflection of who you are, what others would see if everything else was stripped away and all that was left was what you stand for. Albert Einstein often insisted that he had no special gifts, except perhaps his curiosity, focus, and persistence. In other words, the all-time poster child for genius pointed to his personal values as the source of his accomplishment! When we take our values to heart and express them in the smallest details of our lives, great accomplishment and success will always follow.

Take a moment now to reflect on the values that are the bedrock of your belief system. Some common values include trust, integrity, generosity, inclusiveness, fairness, loyalty, fortitude, steadfastness, and independence. These are just a few of the many values that shape our worldview and are at the center of who we are and the choices we make. Values are also at the core of your soft assets and will be the motivators that keep you focused on what matters most to you.

PLAYBOOK

Brainstorm Your Values

From among the sixty general values listed below, circle ten that you consider to be important to you or approximately represent what you care about or what motivates you.

Accountability	Competence	Environment
Achievement	Competition	Ethics
Advancement	Cooperation	Excellence
Adventure	Creativity	Fame
Affection	Curiosity	Freedom
Arts	Decisiveness	Friendships
Beauty	Democracy	Goodness
Caring	Economic security	Growth
Change	Effectiveness	Having a family
Community	Efficiency	Helping other people

Helping society	Mastery	Reputation
Honesty	Meaningful work	Responsibility
Independence	Peace	Security
Inner harmony	Persistence	Self-respect
Integrity	Physical challenge	SerenityIntellectual
status	Pleasure	Sophistication
Involvement	Power	Spirituality
Justice	Privacy	Stability
Knowledge	Prosperity	Status
Leadership	Public service	Truth
Love	Recognition	

Now look at the ten you've circled and imagine that you can choose only five that represent your values best. From the five that remain, choose the three that absolutely most closely represent what you value and believe in. Here's a place to start refining the language that best describes your values.

Values seem to have been one of the "it" subjects of the last twenty-five years. *In Search of Excellence,* Tom Peters's seminal book, started the ball rolling on the subject of values in the workplace. Religious leaders speak of family values, and national leaders speak of moral values. And most recently there has been a lot of thought about the notion of intrinsic (Type I) and extrinsic (Type X) values and motivations.

If you take a moment to think about the successful people in your life, you will realize that some have been leading their lives either focused on intrinsic value or in search of extrinsic value. The author Daniel Pink describes people as Type I (Intrinsic) people, who are intrinsic seekers, or Type X (Extrinsic) people, who are extrinsic seekers. Type I concerns itself with the inherent enjoyment of life, while Type X's main motivation and value are external gains. Those whom you know who have done well motivated by their passions have been motivated by intrinsic value.

A clever definition of intrinsic value is when you do something for the enjoyment of "it"—whatever "it" is. That means you live your life driven by what you adore, value, and care about most for no other reason than the act itself. Folks driven by intrinsic value are not motivated by money and tend to self-actualize their full potential much sooner than others do. What is also interesting about intrinsic value–driven folks is that they play more, live longer, are healthier, and usually end up wealthier in the long run. I believe intrinsic seekers today are the true modern geniuses. Think of Richard Branson, Tony Robbins, Oprah Winfrey, and Steve Jobs; they are all motivated and have been energized to do what they love to do for its own sake—and as a result have never had to chase a dollar. Extrinsic value is value driven by external gain and reward. If you are of this tribe, which is solely motivated by material quest, you are operating from extrinsic value.

Many of the values we think define us are values we were encouraged to adopt rather than those we chose for ourselves. Your dad taught you to be frugal. Your favorite teacher encouraged you to be thorough. If you think about what you really love and what truly motivates you and align yourself with those intrinsic values, you will discover your ability to work patiently toward mastery and to work autonomously with great satisfaction. Ultimately you will find that this sets you up for sustainable success. Believe me when I tell you that living by intrinsic value—defined as living a life filled and prioritized by activities that give you pleasure and engage in for the inherent satisfaction of the activity rather than for some other reason—will transform your life from top to bottom. "The good news," according to Dan Pink, "is that Type Is are made, not born—and that Type I behavior leads to stronger performance, greater health, and higher overall well-being."

This Type I idea matters because it is your connection between what you value and what drives you. If you haven't realized it by now, those drivers are directly connected and in many cases are the same. Pink's masterpiece is called *Drive* for a reason; intrinsic value and the elements that contribute to sustaining a life around what really matters is what will motivate you toward autonomy, mastery, and purpose. And isn't that what every genius aspires to?

PLAYBOOK

Personal Graffiti

Grab a piece of paper and "tag up" or sketch out the ideas, activities, people, or places that truly motivate you. Think about how much time you've devoted to those things in the last week. How many of the six ingredients we've just discussed are involved in any of those motivations? Now you are starting to get a sense of where you are on a personal genius scale.

Each of the six ingredients (skills, strengths, expertise, passions, creative abilities, and values) you've just explored within yourself all contribute in a unique way to your genius, and none is more important than the other. What you've probably uncovered about yourself while going through this evaluation is that you may be tilting too far toward the hard or too far toward the soft. For example, many of my executive clients have invested 90 percent of their time, energy, and mind share on their hard assets and their soft assets are weak, scrawny, and completely underutilized. For some of the entrepreneurs I advise, the opposite is true. They are creative self-indulgers who haven't invested enough in their hard assets and wonder why they are broke. The art and science of practical genius are the mastery and maintenance of purpose for both your heart and mind.

FINALLY, IDENTIFY THE PLACE WHERE YOUR HARD AND SOFT ASSETS MEET

Now that you've moved through an audit of your hard and soft assets, let's look at where they intersect—at that sweet spot where your practical genius resides. When I think of contemporaries who are making a significant impact on society, I realize that many of them—whether they are business leaders, writers, entrepreneurs, artists, technologists, designers, or scientists—are operating at the unique intersection of their hard and soft human assets.

Consider the musical behemoth Bono; the editor-in-chief of *The Huffington Post*, Arianna Huffington; the performer Lady Gaga; Chris Anderson, the curator of the TED Conference; or the architect Zaha Hadid. They are all great examples of folks living at their other G-spot, using all their ingredients to do extraordinary things. To be precise, they are living fully realized, utterly and comprehensively engaged lives. Those people don't have it all—they are making it all happen for themselves by running on the curl of the big wave of all of their human assets. What's their secret?

In order to be an effective influencer, forward-thinking leader, or change agent, you must tackle today's problems in a very different way than was required even twenty years ago. Today there is no room for being one-dimensional, because today's challenges are three-dimensional and require three-dimensional approaches. Life and business were simpler back in the day, but with the technological revolution and the global economic downturn, today we are experiencing high-definition, 3-D challenges, and you don't have to wear those funky glasses to notice both the plentitude of opportunities and the complicated challenges we face. Gone are the days where business could be tackled without empathy. Gone are the days where technological innovation could exist without the prioritization of human psychology. Contemporary geniuses today are tackling problems by connecting the unlikely assets within themselves and bringing them to the solution, meshing all that contributes to their genius capital.

An article in the *Harvard Business Review* discussed a study that showed that "strategic thought entails at least as much emotional intelligence as it does IQ." Using functional magnetic resonance imaging (MRI) to measure brain activity in a study of managers in a Wharton executive MBA program, they found that the best strategic performers showed less neural activity in the prefrontal cortex than in the areas associated with "gut" responses, empathy, and emotional intelligence. Call me crazy, but I see this as proof that integrating the heart and mind does indeed produce better strategists, problem solvers, and bottom-line geniuses.

How many times have you heard "I work to live rather than I live to work" or my other favorite, "I do what I am good at rather than what I love to do." To find your other G-spot, the place where practical genius is born, you have to let go of those ideas and begin to bust out of those limited boxes. How can you do this? You take all your human assets and combine them to form your new currency, your new operating system, and your new way of understanding what you do, how you do it, and why you do it. *This is your path to practical genius.*

Do you think this kind of a life is a fantasy? Is it a pipe dream to find fulfillment *and* financial success in the world of work today, especially in these challenging economic times? I'm here to tell you that it's not impossible. In fact, I'm telling you that it's *imperative* that you integrate these different parts of yourself into a unified whole. All it requires is a bit of reprogramming.

Living a life at the intersection of who you are—professionally and personally—and meshing both worlds into one requires new approaches toward your work and your life. Operating from a place of practical genius requires you to bring all of yourself to everything you do, whether it be running an organization, parenting, or community organizing. It's a multidimensional approach, which will enable you to use your divine perspective right alongside your technological abilities. It will allow you to use humor right alongside your management abilities. It will allow you operationalize complex processes with the aid of nuanced creativity. Energy, passion, personality, intimacy, and many other personal attributes that were looked upon as inappropriate in your professional existence will not only be proper, but will become some of your most effective tools.

THE FORMULA

By now you are probably wondering, how am I going to find that sweet spot? Here is my practical three-step plan to get you there.

First, you have to make the decision to marry the hard and soft sides of who you are. Second, once that commitment is made, you need to quit cheating on any of the six assets that comprise your genius. The third and final step is to identify new and stimulating experiences and relationships that will allow you to explore and expand the facets of yourself you may not even know exist. I consider this step the "foreplay." Give yourself the permission to experiment and taste new experiences. At first you may not know where to start, but listen to your intuition, which sends you loud messages and hints all the time.

For some of my creative clients, this means taking a business class or learning a new language. For some of my executives, this means learning how to salsa dance. Reach to the farthest edges, the fringes of your curiosities, and spend some serious time there. Go for the activities that will stimulate places in you that are currently underutilized. If you are a logical, analytical type, spend some time with activities that engage your creative abilities, passions, or values. If you are a creative type, focus on a hard skill you really need to move your creative passions forward. Eventually, a more balanced, more engaged, more brimming-with-possibility you will emerge. Don't keep doing what you have been doing—change it! This foreplay is critical to reaching your other G-spot.

Yes, it takes practice and a great deal of trial and error, but over time an improved you, a more complete you, will crystalize. I have seen this happen with every client I have coached and with members of my audiences in corporate training. Once you begin to experiment with the practical genius model, you will begin to enjoy a new kind of openness to your own existence, and once the doors are open, your world will change.

For example, I coached a financial expert for a whole year, and by the end of our work together, he had realized that the place he could put all his assets into play was as a spiritual adviser. Here was an extremely accomplished finance professional who had spent his entire career in finance and his private, personal time as a student of scripture, and his revelation was the place where both of those parts of him met. So he decided to keep his job in finance and at the same time launched his own spiritual coaching practice. The result was a happier husband, a more productive professional, and a well-centered practical genius who takes dance lessons with his wife, coaches and encourages folks from his "congregation," and puts his financial expertise to great purpose every day.

In my own life I have learned through practice, persistence, and playing hard that in order to experience practical genius you must learn where it will flourish best. Once I identified the intersection of my talents, strengths, and skills with my values, passions, and creative abilities, I realized almost immediately that my practical genius came to life onstage as a high-impact speaker. Through storytelling, provocative imagery, smart content, practical advice, and good music, I was able to exude and leverage all of my human capital at once. This realization—or rather, actualization—was nothing short of a revelation, a moment of perfect grace and, yes, genius.

Take all your human assets, and be prepared for them to become your new currency, your new operating system, your new way of understanding what you do, how you go about doing it, and why. Be ready to upgrade your approach toward the personal and the professional and let it all hang out. Accept the contradictions and let go of the fear, and I promise that not only will you be happier but you will attract much more to your life, both qualitatively and quantitatively.

Practice

Aristotle once said, "We are what we repeatedly do. Excellence, then, is not an act but a habit." I have to be clear that practical genius is about deliberate practice and painstakingly hard work. Unless the hard work is also your play, you're not going to get anywhere. Finding your genius and deciding to work on it aggressively won't be easy, so if you're looking for shortcuts or easy solutions, go find another book.

Study Yourself

Take time to study yourself. Deeply investigate what makes you you. Be mindful not to edit this body of knowledge; just accept it, all of it—the good, the bad, the needs-improvement areas, and, most important, the fun spaces in your life that have been neglected. Build the knowledge of self-understanding about what you love, how you want to live, and what you can't live without. Become an expert in *you*. It's difficult to understand your full potential if you haven't studied yourself thoroughly. So get to it!

Explore

Explore your possibilities. Over the course of this book, I want you to indulge your curiosities. Google the activities you are curious about but haven't dared to try. Try something new. Plan an escapade. You can't go about identifying your genius without a shot of adventure, so please don't sit still while you turn the pages of this book. Do one small thing everyday, even if it's just walking your dog on a completely new route. The idea is to get your head outside itself and stimulate your senses through dashes of adventure. Over time the outcome will be increased self-awareness and a better idea of who you really are and what you have the potential of unleashing within yourself. Dare to discover something new about yourself.

Experiment

When you bring opposites together or juxtapose things, magic happens. Bring the unlikely together in your life, and experiment. For example, take a painting class during your lunch break. Read a book in a category you know nothing about. Venture into a grocery store in a diverse neighborhood you have never ventured into and buy something you've never eaten before. Become a lab rat for your own transformation, one small experiment at a time.

Play

In order to discover new truths about your genius, *you must play more.* This can mean carving out time for adult play, such as golf or a night out at the ballet, or really diving into playtime with your children. Play every day. Develop play habits. Jump rope. Skip down your driveway. Dress up with your children or fly a kite. I have a friend who plays like this: she gets her kids to open the phone book and randomly choose a name. Then they take turns making up a whole tale around the name, complete with physical description, an elaborate backstory, and a crazy misadventure the person must endure. This kind of play never fails to limber and lighten you up. Play is critical to the pursuit of genius. Whatever play looks like to you, do it.

PORTRAIT OF A PRACTICAL GENIUS

Always on the hunt for geniuses whose hard and soft assets mix elegantly, I was tickled to meet Mariano, a true practical genius. Mariano is an Argentine musician and IT executive who has found his other G-spot, the place where the professional and the personal get serious together.

"I moved to London three years ago, and it was only in a new country that I gave myself permission to be one Mariano rather than the two people I was in Argentina. I had been a high-level IT wonk by day and a raging musician by night, and those two worlds never met. I didn't realize that this divide was pulling me into a depression. It was only when I moved to London and made the decision to connect the most important parts of myself that my life completely opened up for me in ways I never ever imagined possible. I outed my creative side at my company and began to use my creative assets to expand my IT life. This called for me to take a more relaxed approach to my work life, and the change was dramatic. My quality of life improved, my work productivity went through the roof, and my music really began to evolve. By consciously bringing together all of the assets related to my work and creative life, everything I did became more intense and colorful, and more rewarding, too.

"For example, performing and sharing my music with large audiences gave me greater confidence sharing, presenting, and participating in meetings at work. I learned through my own experience that performing arts really help you become more aware of yourself and help your confidence and ability to work with other people. My understanding of the intricacies of technology helped me create and enhance the music I was making, quite literally. By incorporating a few laptops, which play samples as background, and creating a sequence, which takes signals from my guitar, the result is an amazing new sound."

SUMMING UP

The road to practical genius begins with the extraction of six key ingredients that contribute to who you are and the embrace and acceptance of all sides of yourself. The war between your identities will come to a halt right inside your genius zone.

Practical genius is the intersection between what you love and what you do best. This sweet spot is where the professional and the personal joyfully mesh and is the essence of your practical genius.

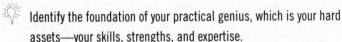 Identify the foundation of your practical genius, which is your hard assets—your skills, strengths, and expertise.

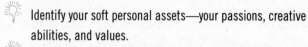 Identify your soft personal assets—your passions, creative
abilities, and values.

Identify the sweet spot where the hard and soft assets meet.

Now you're at that special place where the cultivation of your personal power begins. It's not enough to know where your other G-spot lives; you have to get out there and do something with it. We start by giving your genius a voice and a story. Keep reading.

MY STORY!

EXPRESS YOUR GENIUS

It's Time to Tell Your Story

One of the great benefits of being a human being (as opposed to being an emu, for instance) is the endless ways we have to express ourselves. Lucky us. Language, music, art, dance—we don't have to say a thing, but we can give expression to a whole wide world of truth, experience, and feelings. The more evolved the species, the more sophisticated the means of expression—or so the story goes.

In fact, whereas animals use every expressive tool in their toolbox (screeches and howls, glances and gestures, touch and chase) for practical reasons of survival, we human beings are notorious for ignoring most of our expressive capabilities, choosing instead to use a few of the simplest tools (or blunt objects) even at the risk of spending a lifetime being misunderstood or unappreciated.

Let me be clear: this is not an option for the practical genius.

Living as a practical genius requires that you use all the tools at your disposal—every letter of the alphabet, every color, every note, every shape and texture of the human experience—to give expression to your genius. If you can't express it, it might as well not be there.

I think that generally folks believe that if they are reasonably communicative and attempt to make themselves clear, they're doing a good job of expressing themselves to others. But I'm here to tell you that what you're doing now isn't enough. The good news: I can teach you another way to express yourself, and I can show you how to turn your self-expression into a genius asset of tremendous proportions.

To begin with, what comes out of your mouth is only a small fraction of what you communicate to others. The expression on your face, what you're wearing, the way you carry your body, even which seat you choose at a conference table tells people something about you. You actually express yourself all day long, although I'd guess you rarely do it with a particular purpose, and you certainly don't tell the whole story.

That's what it is, you know—a story. There's a story you're telling about yourself as you move through the world. It may not be the story you mean to tell. And even if it's the story you'd choose for yourself, I guarantee you're not telling it as well as you should.

I have a friend who goes to parties and always says to people she's just met, "Nice to meet you. So what's your story?" She says people almost never know where to start their story, usually falling back on how they know the host of the party or what they do for a living. That's not a story! That's a wasted opportunity to express your genius.

When I ask you, "What's your story?," I want your answer to make me understand your narrative; I want to hear the vocabulary and themes that reflect your values; and I want to see your "illustrations," the visual expressions of the genius of you. Like me, the people you work with, play with, and live with *want* to know your story. We want to hear it every time we interact with you, because it conveys your authenticity and helps to increase the value and meaning of our relationship over time. Yet how much do we leave out of our stories? How much do we leave on the table or never leverage in our relationships because we're not telling our genius story?

In this chapter, I'm going to take you through a step-by-step process of identifying and telling your own compelling story. You'll learn how to find your unique narrative, identify a few salient themes, illustrate that story with rich details, and share it all with people in a brief two minutes or less. But first I want to explain *why* it's so important for every practical genius to have his or her own story ready to share.

THE "NOTHING"

Remember the 1984 children's film, *The Neverending Story?* It was based on a German fantasy novel about a young boy's quest to save Fantasia, a land without boundaries that was created by the dreams and hopes of mankind. Fantasia was slowly dying as people lost their imaginations and ability to dream to an emptiness and despair that were referred to as the "Nothing."

"People who have no hopes are easy to control," said the servant to the power behind the Nothing. That quote has remained with me since I first heard it at the age of twelve. I think that today many of us are unconsciously falling under the power of the Nothing, abdicating our imaginations and courage to dream and hope and tell our whole stories in the real world. Expressing genius is expressing your hopeful self, the intuitive self that leads with vigorous curiosity. Are you battling the Nothing in your work, seeing just glimmers of your hope only on weekends, when you're free to imagine? Are you surrounded by people who are part of the Nothing, who ignore their own imaginations and don't care about their stories?

Consider how the Nothing has taken over many of the folks you work with. Many professionals walk the halls of organizations in a numb state, robotic in their behavior, believing that sharing their soft assets is "inappropriate." Well, I think censoring creative abilities, values, and passions in the workplace is inappropriate and has contributed to the spreading of the Nothing in many organizations, both big and small.

The Nothing is a powerful analogy to help keep you accountable to a personal form of expression of a contributing, gifting nature. Expressing your genius is a personal quest to vanquish the Nothing. It's about ensuring that the meaning and value of your story are constantly being conveyed, to the benefit of both yourself and others. But first you have to know what your story is.

WHAT'S YOUR STORY?

If your practical genius is the place where your hard and soft assets intersect, the single most important way you leverage that sweet spot is by telling your story. I don't mean a stiff little biography of yourself like this: "My name is Anne, I grew up in the Midwest, now live in Atlanta and work as finance director with Widget Inc. I have two kids, and in my spare time I enjoy my book club." No offense, Anne, but I am neither enchanted by your story nor convinced of your genius. This sorry, one-dimensional elevator pitch just doesn't cut it. I want a story that shows me something true about you. When you think about your story, I want you to ask yourself what that story *looks* like. For that matter, what does it sound like, feel like, and taste like? It needs to have that much texture. So let's dig in.

Take an ordinary day in your life. Have you ever really listened to yourself? What's the internal narrative of your day? What's the game plan you lay out in the locker room (the bathroom, your car)? What are the thought balloons, the notes to self you make throughout the day? How often do you use your internal narrative to prepare for an important meeting?

Expressing your practical genius is not about expressing the limitedness of our personalities or egos but more about expressing wonder of the depths of the oceans of who we are as complex multidimensional creatures. Certainly all of those pieces of information Anne shared above are true. But what if she adapted that flat profile with some of the texture and topography of who she *really* is—say, a cheerful atheist married to an Episcopal priest. Or the Scripps Howard National Spelling Bee champion of 1989. Or a breeder of Rhodesian Ridgebacks. Those aren't details Anne would fling randomly to the wind. They are pieces of the story of her that she should learn how to tell—and that I would *much* rather hear because she just might be a genius I want to know!

Here's your challenge: Take a whole day to note all the instances and ways you tell your story—if at all. What are the signals you send in your ordinary exchanges with people? Is there anything consistent about the way you project yourself to those who populate your day? Do you convey an energy, a sense of contribution, or connections with others that are a reflection of you are across all of your communications? When you e-mail or tweet or update your profiles on any one of a number of digital venues, are you purposefully telling your story—or are you just regurgitating empty bits of information that have no meaning and steal time from you and everyone who reads about you?

THE TWO-MINUTE DRILL

Here's a stunning reality: you have only two minutes to get someone to care about you. That's it. The all-time two-minute drill. That means you don't have the luxury of indulging in small talk or gossip or gripey nonsense when you engage with people every day—whether you know them or not. So if you waste your two minutes on sports or the weather or even your kids (God bless them), you've burned through your currency with that person and you should not expect to get another chance to impress your truly valuable, authentic story on him or her again. Game over.

When I train executives to express their genius, the first exercise I ask them to do is to go up to someone they don't know and make that person care about them in two minutes. You would be shocked to see how many highly trained, exquisitely educated, massively accomplished managers and executives stumble through this conversation. Often they have no idea how to initiate a conversation of substance and meaning. They have no concept of the story they need to tell and less of a sense of what the other person needs or wants to hear. Trust me—this is painful to watch.

During a corporate training session on expressing practical genius, a senior vice president whom I will call Mark decided to hold on to his resistance and play it safe. He chose to talk about football and the life-shattering disappointment he had felt when his team lost the previous weekend. What didn't register with Mark was that the young manager he was speaking with had committed entirely to the exercise and had shared with Mark the fact that he was adopted as a child. The manager found Mark's lack of sincerity and inability to open up a trust buster and a turnoff. Mark told the wrong story, people.

There's a moment in this exercise when the discomfort begins to diminish because some of the natural storytellers come to the surface. Some tell childhood stories; other share short stories of triumph or funny stories or stories with a pulsing heart the other person is powerless to ignore.

I love this exercise. After everyone is done, I ask the participants to identify the best stories they have heard, and this inevitably leads to an active discussion that reveals that many have worked for years together but have never heard the others' stories. This exercise can be liberating for many, but also a wake-up call to how powerful your story can be if you really know what your story is and know how to tell it.

One of my favorites was told by an architect who was trying his two-minute drill on me. "Have you ever slept outdoors?" he began, to which I responded "Not in many years." He proceeded to share that he'd been looking for a way to get a better understanding of the environment in his own neighborhood for a green project he was working on. So he decided to camp out in his urban backyard for ten days, pretty much just to see if he could do it. To his surprise, he learned a great deal from his experience, a real treasure trove of insights and impressions that completely changed his approach to his concept for his green project. For example, his greatest takeaway from the experience was that the design of the project should not only be green but create functional outdoor workspace. His story was short, simple, and beautifully visual, leaving a picture of the type of man I felt quite certain he was. I especially loved how his story revealed the connection between his authenticity (who he is) and his capacity (what he is capable of doing).

Hard-asset types often tell résumé/job interview kinds of stories or play it safe with small talk, which is just that—small in its impact. I don't know who exactly started the "small-talk standard" of expressing oneself in insignificant ways—entertaining small topics such as the weather, sports, or traffic—but I find it unacceptable. In fact, I believe small talk and the shallowness that comes with it create more boundaries and contribute to numbness of expression, one of the contributing factors to why so few of us have the meaningful conversations we should be having on a daily basis.

How about we set a "no small talk" rule for all practical geniuses to live by? When I meet someone for the first time and he begins to engage me on a small, safe level, I immediately look for a way to prompt him toward sharing something he really cares about rather than the evening weather report. Expressing genius is never about frivolous, meaningless, safe conversations that just fill the air. Think of every conversation—even shorties—as a chance to grow your genius and contribute to that growth in someone else.

Soft-asset types tell the smushier creative stuff about who they *really* are, as if to make excuses for the hard part of themselves they have to hold their noses to live with. But in the end, artists tell art stories. Moms tell mom stories. Lawyers tell lawyer stories. The question is, why do we continue to frame our stories by how we spend our time or, more precisely, how we make a living? We speak our professions well and are experts at sharing the details of our careers, but ask most people to share their passions or the unplugged version of their lives and most can't—because they haven't had much practice at sharing *meaning*.

The goal in expressing your genius is to reveal it without silencing the hard side for the soft or vice versa. What will help you avoid that tendency is to try not to share from a place of assumptions, labels, and societal expectations of what is and isn't appropriate to share. Remove those barriers and practice being honest and transparent, and whoever is listening will feel a sense of trust in return. Try this, I mean it. You will be shocked how easy it is, once you commit to quit talking about nonsense. The result will be edifying engagement, and most people will gladly follow your lead.

See where I'm going with this? This two-minute drill reveals whether you have a story at all, whether your story reflects a bias toward your soft or hard assets, and whether you let small talk and minutiae get in the way of the story you should be telling.

By the end of this chapter, you'll have all the components you need to craft your own compelling two-minute genius story. But first let me share my own story with you.

YOU'RE ALWAYS TELLING YOUR STORY

When you begin to understand that every exchange you have with another person is an exercise in telling your story, you're on to something. Gone are the days when you could hide the personal you behind the professional you. Here forever are the days when you project a positive, powerful, purposeful narrative that puts your genius out there in the world.

Why does your story matter? Because it tells the truth. Because it inspires, explains, or connects you with someone else. Because it is powerful, free, persuasive, natural, entertaining, memorable, and, above all, authentic.

Let's look at mine. Here's the story I tell about where I am right now in my life:

One day when I was in the third grade at my Catholic grammar school, I remember children being pulled out of my classroom and taken to a much nicer room down the hall that had beautiful windows and flowers on the windowsills.

I waited patiently for my name to be called to move to that nicer room, which had been designed and designated for the "gifted" students in my class. My name was never called. I went home that day and shared the story of that special room and the flowers in the windows and asked my mother when I would be called to go to that room.

As any good Latina would do, my mother marched into the principal's office the very next morning, demanding to know why her daughter had not been assigned to the new gifted program.

The elderly nun patiently explained to my mother that although I was a sweet, well-mannered child, academically I was average. To a hardworking single mother with the highest hopes for her obviously extraordinary child, that was like a life sentence of disappointment for her and hardship for me.

My mom is a straight shooter, though, and that night she sat me down and recounted her conversation with the principal without mincing too many words. "Gina, this is a class for gifted students, and they think you are average. You will just have to keep trying," she said, struggling to convince me of the truth of that.

As I look back on my educational experience and my professional career, I realize that my challenge has always been to try harder, to do more, to communicate more effectively, to do whatever it takes to get the attention I deserved for the intelligence and creativity and sheer determination that I always knew in my heart I possessed. Yet I learned early on—probably from my wise and loving mother—that I needed always to be ready to crash through the barriers to entry. If I had allowed that nun to frame my story, I would have ended up an average girl with an average life, and I knew even then that that was just not who I am.

I quickly tapped into the power of my own determination, my proud self-identification, and my ability to strategize around just about any kind of adversity. I learned how to master and market my strengths, which got me into Binghamton University and then earned me a full scholarship to Baruch College for a master's degree as a National Urban Fellow. Take that, "gifted program"! Fighting to be sure that others understand exactly who I am and what I'm truly capable of—that is my truth; that is my story.

You may have noticed that my story is about my elementary school principal basically calling me a loser. Yet why isn't that the takeaway of the story?

We've been taught our whole lives to hide our failures. Did you put that D+ spelling quiz up on the refrigerator with a magnet? Do you lead with details of unsuccessful projects or unfavorable job reviews on your résumé? Does your Facebook page exhaustively account for all of your failed romantic relationships? Nope. We learn from an early age how to spin our failures and put a lot of sweet frosting on top to make ourselves more likable, more marketable. And that's a good strategy . . . up to a point.

Martha Beck is one of America's most famous life coaches, but her own life has not been without challenge and heartbreak. She has suffered from fibromyalgia for almost thirty years. She is a mother of three, including a son who has Down syndrome, whom she wrote about in the very moving *Expecting Adam: A True Story of Birth, Rebirth, and Everyday Magic.* She left the close-knit Mormon Church and has written candidly about the sexual abuse she endured as a child. With all of this, Martha has a PhD from Harvard and her own new show on the Oprah Winfrey Network and is "one of the smartest women I know," Oprah says. Her career seemed to benefit from the same recipe of equal parts of heart and mind and is a great example of a woman who walks and talks her practical genius without ever censoring herself.

I think there's a lot to be gained from not only learning from but also sharing publicly our tougher moments. I propose that we stop burying the less triumphant moments of our lives and start letting them play a valuable role in our storytelling. When you're secure enough to out your weaknesses and share a few of your greatest misses, you convey to others that you have no fear. One of my spiritual gurus, Reverend Chris Jackson, always says to reveal your greatest weakness immediately to others to show them that you have nothing to lose. It is only when you have nothing to lose that the magnitude of what you have to gain can fully empower you. "Gina," he told me, "When you reach a place in your life where you are ready to take the risk of telling the truth, that is when life begins teaching you plenty." Listen to your life experiences; your personal truths are filled with rich expression and valuable content.

My story, just like any good two-minute story, consists of four important components—the narrative, the themes, the vocabulary, and the illustrations. I'll break them down for you here, show you how to find these components for yourself and then how to use those components to build your own unique, winning genius story.

The Narrative

Every story has a beginning, a middle, and an end. There's a narrative arc to every tale that allows the listener to be brought along and participate in the emotional transaction that takes place in the telling. Does the story *you're* telling right now have a narrative arc? Or is it a series of random non sequiturs or some kind of self-glorifying highlight reel or worse? This is the stuff that makes the listener look for the exit signs of your conversation. Hell, those kinds of stories can make *you* want to make a run for it yourself.

I have a client, Lauralee, who attempted to sidestep this part of her practical genius learning. She was convinced (and was trying to convince me) that there wasn't a particularly interesting narrative to share about her life. She is a sales executive with a conference planning company, and she believed that the work she was doing in the here and now was the only story anyone needed to hear about her.

But with a little prodding, I discovered that early in her life, Lauralee had been bitten by the travel bug, and in fact she'd traipsed around the world, working with a traveling carnival. Hello! She was a *carnie?* By the time we got to that part of her story, I was hooked.

I think that Lauralee felt that revealing the more carefree part of her early life wouldn't encourage people to take her seriously. But I knew that the opposite was true: this story revealed a kind of adventurous spirit and a passion for travel that would be memorable and inspiring to those who knew her. To inspire Lauralee to reveal her story—her narrative and themes and all the words that could help express her genius—I asked her to choose photos from her many albums that she felt reflected what was distinctive about her life experience. Her two favorite photos were both reflective of the risk taker Lauralee, one riding a camel in Dahab, a Bedouin camp in the Sinai desert, and the other on a bamboo raft floating on a river in Chiang Mai in northern Thailand.

By the time she finished this homework, her entire perspective on her narrative—what she now understood was her *real* story—had changed. Suddenly she saw all of it as clear as day. She had been focusing on telling her safe corporate story (where she'd gone to college, what types of responsibilities she'd tackled at her most recent job) and had ignored the best part of what she had to share.

"I knew that the intrepid nomad was still in me somewhere, but it felt like a long-dormant volcano," said Lauralee when I later asked her about the experience. "Then I met you, and the volcano began to rumble back to life." She hadn't made the connection that her globetrotting past was actually her greatest competitive advantage. As she shifted her story toward her incredible real-life experiences as a modern-day gypsy, she began to grow in her work and her personal life took a bold turn. "I realized that the risk taker was still in me and I just needed to find her again, albeit an older and wiser version."

In the months that followed this exercise, she examined her life and asked herself on a regular basis, "What if I wasn't afraid?" Telling herself a new story (or in her case, a new version of her old, best story), her genius breakthrough started to roll. "My business has since begun to flourish, and I have found a personal joy and balance in my life that was like a buried treasure I once would have traveled around the planet to discover," she told me.

PLAYBOOK

Your Snapshot Moments

You can do this with photographs, as I asked Lauralee to do. Or you can do it by telling stories as answers to the questions below:

 Can you name the all-time greatest moment of your life? What led up to it and what happened next?

What was your biggest "aha" moment, when you learned and experienced something so profound in your life it changed you forever?
What is the wildest thing you have ever done? What made you do it?

Big Fat Hint: In the previous chapter, you identified the spot where your hard and soft assets meet—and your narrative should always take us to that spot. By now you may also have realized that you can have several versions of your story, but they all express, portray, reveal, illustrate, project, and attract others to your genius.

On many levels the narratives we repeat to ourselves and to others frame our ongoing experience, and therefore it's important to share the stories that place your practical genius at the center of the story. I've come to realize that the more you speak your whole truth, the more affirmed your integrated hard and soft assets become.

For example, one of my dearest friends, Katina, is a former marathon runner. By the time she had her second child, she had gained seventy pounds and had gotten to where she couldn't live with herself. She decided to speak out about her fight with sugar addiction and her battle going from a size 2 to a size 18. Katina, whom I've known for twenty years, has always been a fitness freak, and to see her life change physically and emotionally after having children was hard to watch. I knew she had to change her life, and advising her to first address and change her narrative had an enormous impact. I encouraged her to start a fitness blog, and once she started sharing her story with others she began to live a very different life, once again placing fitness at the center of her health and well-being. The result was weight loss, of course, but also more energy and an overall happier, more authentic woman who now teaches others how to incorporate fitness in their lives no matter what their challenges.

Stories change us. If you are sick and tired of hearing yourself sing the same tune, it's because you've become the flat or boring story you've been telling. It's time to look at the ingredients of your genius and make *that* your story. Reveal something new about yourself that you haven't shared with a person. For example, a client recently shared with me and her team that she was heading on a service trip with her church to help rebuild a neighborhood in Haiti. What was exciting about this new tidbit of information was that she had been going to Haiti for ten years and no one knew it. She was surprised to discover that others were interested in what turned out to be the work she cared most about. In fact, one of her French colleagues who had been curious about Haiti for a while decided to join her on the next service trip as an interpreter. Now, *that's* a practical genius story.

The practical genius model works because it can be applied to every aspect of your life, especially when it comes to how you express yourself. The bottom line is that all of you is relevant and you shouldn't continue to walk through life picking and choosing the parts of you to reveal. It's *all* personal.

PLAYBOOK

Another Snapshot Moment

Is there a photograph of you that you come back to again and again because you (and only you) know it expresses every single thing about you? When you look at that photo, what do you see? Do you see your story? Tell yourself the story you see in that photograph.

The Themes

Do you remember the "themes" section of those saved-your-ass-before-your-final-paper-was-due CliffsNotes booklets? The themes tended to be things such as the Coexistence of Good and Evil (*To*

Kill a Mockingbird), the Death of the American Dream (*The Great Gatsby*), Adolescent Alienation (*The Catcher in the Rye*). A theme is the universal idea that rises to the surface of a good story. You should have one or two of those, too. If you know your themes, whatever story you're telling will be connected to the last one and the next one. They'll be unforgettable variations on your musical score.

The themes we unconsciously marry are accurate expressions of who we are and what matters most to us. Not unlike identifying and expressing your values, it is rare to have an occasion to name your themes. But themes are critical to your genius story, so let's figure out what they are.

Get out your résumé and try to read between the lines, the way a prospective employer would. That intense business development job you had with a start-up? The two years you spent teaching fifth graders in the Bronx with Teach for America after college? **Fearlessness Builds Character.**

The trajectory from an urban neighborhood development director to chief diversity officer of a major corporation? **Leads with Beliefs.**

Next, do a review of the milestones of your life. Were you first in your family to graduate from college but became a social worker instead of a banker as your mother would have preferred? Do you volunteer with a community music program even though you can't read a lick of music? These milestones bring you to approximately the same themes.

Your themes tend to be descriptors, including adjectives and adverbs, and should encompass all sides of you. And they should certainly reflect your values. For example, I had an amazing intern, Atalia Aron, who was both a talented artist and a scientist. She has two master's degrees, one in international business and the second in bioengineering, and is a true logical left-brainer who also possesses an amazing talent for painting. For years her themes felt jumbled to her and it was difficult for her to identify ways to marry her artistic passion and strengths in the sciences. To help her accept both, we worked on a tagline to help quiet down the inner battle between the soft and hard sides of herself. "A scientific mind of artistic design" is what we eventually landed on during one of our weekly painting classes together. (She taught me how to paint.) This tagline—her theme—became her personal tagline on everything from her e-mail signature to the header of her résumé.

The theme is the thread that connects all the chapters or versions of your story. Remember my gifted-class story? My themes in this case are Fierce Determination and Adversity Is an Asset. Every time I tell my stories, my themes are like powerful little "remember this chick" thought balloons over the head of the person I'm talking to. Do you have some of that?

Note that you must select your themes wisely and selfishly, and understand that you have to invest in their growth, reinforce their truth, and nurture your own ability to deliver on them in real time. This is also known as being prepared to walk the walk on your practical genius. If you don't do it, you starve your genius of oxygen and it dies on the vine. If you *do* do it, your themes become blogs, creative ventures, community partnerships, profitable businesses, kick-ass conferences, masterpiece speeches, spellbinding adventures, op-eds and lectures that change people's lives, and deep-into-the-night discussions that sustain you like the air you breathe. Top that.

The Vocabulary

All good messaging begins with the truth. And the words you choose to represent your genius spell out your truth. To begin to refine your story, I would ask you first to put away the language of your parents and your childhood, put away the language of your company or your circle of friends. Your story requires a vocabulary that is unique to you, that sustains and supports your narrative, expresses and supports your themes, and provides a perspective for the way your story is illustrated.

Your vocabulary is related to, but distinct from, your narrative, themes, and illustrations. The keywords in your genius vocabulary are uniquely yours. So what are they? Well, if Fierce Determination is one of my themes, "resourceful," "vision-driven," and "boundless" are a few of my vocabulary words. Those are the terms that describe my practical genius and are the action words that make my story a part of my genius practice, every single day.

I discovered my unique vocabulary through my writing. Writing is my greatest passion as well as my greatest challenge, so I really work at it. Through journaling, writing letters to myself and others, and the daily work of writing, I have discovered my vocabulary. These words are the recurring notes in the song of me that I see in everything I write.

Another important resource in identifying your vocabulary is being an active reader and reading everything you can get your hands on. It's about really consuming and absorbing all content, whether it's graffiti on the side of a building, a good novel, or an op-ed you read in the newspaper on your way to work. Read with a mind toward actively searching for the words that don't just speak *to* you but truly speak *of* you. Once you become conscious of this process, a core collection of words that resonate with and reflect you will form. They can be found in a menu, an ad, a verse of scripture. The more you excavate in this way, the more you will see the trends emerge in the words that find you.

These words—whether spoken, written, or silently acknowledged in the quiet of our own minds—really do shape who we become. For me, change has always started with my vocabulary. When you are purposeful and select the words that become your vocabulary, you are using them to jet-fuel your trajectory into the future. When you let the words form around what you have allowed yourself to become by attrition, well, that's another story. The words you pick versus the words that pick you? Hmmm. Let's see. I'll take the words *I* pick!

Identify your words. Commit them to your heart. Live them every day. Make sure they are the action words of your story and give heart and soul and energy to your themes.

PLAYBOOK

Scavenger Hunt

If you really have an empty word bank, begin identifying the words and phrases you own by grabbing a few of your favorite periodicals and highlighting the words that move you, excite you, or just scream, "Yes, that's me!" Write each of those words or phrases on an index card, and spread them out on a table. Move them around, change the order, try to find the hierarchy of meaning to you. Collect those words into the start of a vocabulary log (or a vocablog!) that you can continue to tweak, refine, and add to.

The Illustrations

The illustrations in your story are the visual bits and pieces that reinforce, educate, entertain, and otherwise help to make your story compelling.

I'm a proud, card-carrying member of the visualization movement. My favorite places in corporate America today are conference rooms where graffiti covers the walls, illustrating the brainstorming, strategic planning, and complex problem solving that happen when smart people are in that room. In this setting, visual note takers "transcribe" the dialogue to provide another dimension of meaning to the participants. I am in awe of the people who are able to make this visual leap because I have seen the power it has to transform the way people think about their work.

GINA RUDAN

GINA, SELF-PORTRAIT

GINA, SELF-PORTRAIT

I'm not an artist, nor are most of the executives and managers I work with. But the tools of art are tremendously valuable in the process of developing, refining, and ultimately illustrating our stories. I keep sketch pads, charcoal pencils, and big fat erasers always at the ready. Having the gear isn't going to turn me from a wordy person into an artsy person. But it does remind me of the necessity to illustrate my thinking while I work, and over time it has helped me develop a visual habit and sensibility that are tremendous assets. I have become an avid collector of colors and shapes, photographs and symbols, diagrams and icons. My illustrations are unique to me, but I am endlessly inspired and energized by the illustration of genius I see all around me every day.

David Sibbet is a visual visionary, a founding partner of Grove Consultants International and the author of *Visual Meetings*. David says that if thinking and visualizing is a process, the simplest thing you can do is keep a visual journal to force yourself to try to apply a graphic to breakthrough ideas you have while you work. Though this seemed like a baby step to me (and a painful one at that, for someone who's not an artist), he convinced me that over time I would be able to go back to my journals and see patterns in my illustrations that would allow me to gauge my growth spurts or identify where I was stuck. Damn, was he right.

PLAYBOOK

Self-Portrait

Sketch a six-box grid on a big piece of poster paper. Each box represents an ingredient of your practical genius—your passions, values, and creative abilities and your strengths, skills, and expertise. In each box, place images or symbols or swatches of color or any other visuals you think represent your unique genius in this area. This is an exercise that should take place over time. When the boxes are full (and you won't be able to stop adding to them, BTW), you will be looking at a self-portrait of your practical genius that will astonish and inspire you.

THE ART OF STORYTELLING

My grandmother Jovita is one of the greatest storytellers I have ever known. Part of her magic is in the way she draws you into the intimacy of her stories, which are often about when she was a young girl growing up in Puerto Rico. This is a woman who was never allowed to go to school and still cannot read or write. Yet she is a natural wordsmith and can take me from shock to laughter to tears in a single stroke. It is also the cadence of her delivery that makes it work.

There are three things she does when she tells a story that I learned from her. First, take your audience someplace else. Get them to use their imaginations to go on your journey with you. If your story causes the imagination switch to turn on, you're halfway home. Second, make your audience run the gamut of emotions with you. Plug them in to your power source. Finally, always tell a story that has resonance and meaning for the audience. It's the ultimate leave-behind.

What I really learned from my grandmother is both the value of an authentic genius story and how important it is to know how to tell it. This is a gift, to be sure, and she's living proof of that. But there are a few simple ways we can tell our stories better.

Edit, Edit, Edit

As I have learned from my writing experience, everything I want to say can be said better with less. It's true. Less is always more. And so it goes for the story you want to tell. Don't get bogged down in minutiae or blow-by-blows that distract from your message. Be concise, clear, and consistent. But don't skimp on the details that make the story yours.

For example, when I tell my elementary school story, one small detail that resonates every single time is this: "As any good Latina would do, my mother marched into the principal's office the very next morning." This detail is kind of funny but very easy to picture and makes a strong emotional connection with my audience. But just so you know, that sentence was edited about a thousand times and ways before it was just what it needed to be. Play with every word of your story to make it tight and right.

The fact that you edit and practice your story doesn't make it less authentic or real. It just means you care enough about it to get it right, to be telling exactly the story you mean to tell. Being deliberate is genius; being random is not.

Listen Up

Believe it or not, being a good listener is one of the most important qualities of being a good storyteller. Be an active listener, and the active listeners in your audience will respond in kind. Be thoughtful and generous about timing. It takes patience, consideration, tolerance, and discipline to move smoothly between listening and speaking. But the impact of your story will increase exponentially as you master the rhythms and the give-and-take of conversation.

Listening is one of the most important skills you can have, and today, with the abundance and overflow of messages and communication, I think our ability to really listen to one another is in peril. How well you listen has a major impact on your practical genius at home, on the job, and also on the quality of your relationships with others.

RAMP UP YOUR LISTENING SKILLS

 First, there's the simple rule: Pay attention to whoever is speaking to you, period. Put down the BlackBerry, give them your undivided attention, and fully absorb and acknowledge the message. To give speakers confidence that they are being heard, look at them directly and avoid being distracted by anything. Anything!

 Quality listening can be hampered by noise, which can be aural or visual. What's going on outside the window on a nice day or a hot waitress walking by, for example, can be classified as noise. When you care about a conversation—and practical geniuses care about *all* of them—look for a quiet place to talk where you can invest yourself in the exchange.

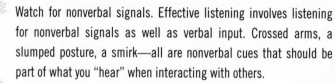 Watch for nonverbal signals. Effective listening involves listening for nonverbal signals as well as verbal input. Crossed arms, a slumped posture, a smirk—all are nonverbal cues that should be part of what you "hear" when interacting with others.

To avoid making incorrect assumptions, you should paraphrase what you hear. Summarize what you've heard, and ask if you understand correctly. That's "active listening" in a nutshell.

Watch your filters. Some stories can easily become misunderstood as a result of our filters, assumptions, and judgments, which is unfortunate but true. Be open and try to listen without judging the person. Don't be afraid to ask questions at the end of the conversation; you want to make sure that the speaker knows you understood their message.

Voice Lessons

Your voice can convey your authority and authenticity—or not—more than just about anything else about you. What a shame if you had the world's best story to tell and no one got it because all they could hear was your squeaky, nervous, uncommanding voice? Your best voice is natural, not stagey or singsongy or stiff. Be who you are, even when you're telling the most important story of your life! A solid, deliberate, unwavering voice says, "You should listen to this. It'll be worth your while." A weak, wobbly voice says, "I'm not sure about this. Maybe you should be listening to someone else."

I remember sitting in a meeting where one particular female executive was pitching a group of executives, and I could hear her voice rising and even cracking uncomfortably. I felt her pain and wanted to shake her out of it in the bathroom during a break, but it wasn't the right time for me to give her a reality check so I had to bear her presentation while watching everyone else grinding their teeth in response. It was painful, and the saddest part is that she was not aware of it at all. She was a talented, smart woman with great ideas, but her lack of ability to reach her audience confidently had a negative impact on her credibility and reputation.

PLAYBOOK

Hear Your Own Voice

Use your phone or computer or an audio recorder to capture the sound of yourself speaking. Record yourself reading a poem or reading a newspaper article out loud. Even better, set yourself up to record a business telephone call. You will learn so much from what you hear.

If you have what people call a "squeaky voice," a speech therapist can help you. A solid, deliberate, unwavering voice is critical to expressing your genius. The author Naomi Wolf once told me, "Speak to me in statements, not questions," and I've never forgotten that advice. When you speak in a questioning style and your sentences "curl up" at the end, you are the student. When you speak in a statement style, with steadiness and confidence, you are the teacher.

Remember, you can have the smartest things to say, but if no one can hear you or understand you, it doesn't do you any good. Project! Enunciate! Speak with purpose! A recent University of California study observed several small work groups focused on a similar task. After the entire group viewed videotapes of the work sessions, they agreed that those who spoke up were probably higher in general intelligence, while quieter team members were tagged as conventional or uncreative.

Record audio of yourself next time you speak in front of a group. Then tell me if you sound like a smart guy or a dud. Or ask a close colleague for a brutally honest assessment of your speaking skills. If you're not being heard, you need to know it—and correct it.

BODY TALK

When I speak, I think of what I'm saying as the melody of a song and what my body is doing as the harmony. When your voice and body work together to express what you intend, it's music. When your mouth is doing one thing and your body's doing another, it's dissonance. Your eyes, your hands, your posture, every gesture—they are all powerful punctuation to your story. The pioneering research of the interpersonal communication expert Albert Mehrabian showed that just 7 percent of our attitudes and beliefs are conveyed to others through words we speak, while 38 percent comes from our tone of voice and 55 percent from our facial and other body expressions. Yikes! All the more important to get our stories synced up with our voices and bodies.

Be mindful of the physical messages you send and the ones you receive from others. They can be highly effective when used carefully. For example, Reverend Chris Jackson of Unity on the Bay speaks to his congregation with his eyes along with his words. His movement, his tone, and his powerful glances are always in sync, and he is one of the best messengers I've ever witnessed. By watching him, I've learned how to dance with my audience with my eyes.

The opposite of this delicate physical choreography also exists. Those who communicate loudly, in a sometimes vulgar or impolite way, with their body language are often engaged in something known as "micromessaging." For example, one time I was meeting a president of a marketing agency for lunch, and throughout the entire lunch he kept getting up and excusing himself from the table to speak with other folks who happened also to be in the restaurant. The first time it happened, I thought he had just bumped into an old friend, but the second and third times he left the table, I knew I was being told I didn't matter. During the few minutes he did share his attention with me at the table, he continued to scope out the room for more acquaintances. I knew I would never do business with that guy and actually gave his partner, who was a complete gentleman trying to overcompensate for his counterpart's rudeness, my feedback on the entire experience. I never received an apology and had to acknowledge that the entire experience was a strong example of micromessaging. Micromessages are subtle and not-so-subtle signals that represent the core of the message someone is sending, and they usually demonstrate inclusion or exclusion. The warm or frequent touch of a person's forearm during conversation or a steady, locked-in, paying-attention-to-only-you gaze are examples of inclusive type of micromessages.

Nonverbal communication matters most, and if our body language says something different from our words, listeners will believe the nonverbal. This leads me to the power of touch.

A TOUCH OF GENIUS

Have you realized how far a hug, a kiss hello, or a gentle pat on the shoulder can go? Interpersonal communication is much more than the effective use of verbal language and body language; it also involves touch. A warm touch releases oxytocin, a hormone that helps create a sensation of trust. An article in *The New York Times* described the work of psychologists who have found that momentary touches—whether a high-five or a warm hand on the shoulder—can communicate an even wider range of emotion than gestures or expressions and sometimes do so more quickly and accurately than words.

When it comes to performance, scientists at Berkeley recently analyzed the interactions of professional basketball players and discovered that players who made physical contact with teammates most consistently and longest tended to rate highest on measures of performances and the teams with those players seemed to get the most out of their talent. When it comes to teams and performance, the body interprets a supportive touch as "I'll share the load," which leads to greater collaboration and human investment. Touch is powerful, and all practical geniuses must leverage the power of touch in their own lives. Remember that when it comes to attitudes and beliefs, your body speaks louder than words.

BODY LANGUAGE MADE SIMPLE

Below are some body language basics that are oriented toward communications in the United States.

Share yourself. The best body language tip I have for you is to share yourself in person. In this fast-paced era of e-mail, IM, and text messaging, one universal truth remains: face-to-face is still the most preferred, productive, and powerful medium for expressing genius. Face your audience, make eye contact, be sure your movements are relaxed and natural, and stand tall—all of which are nonverbal signs of credibility and competence.

Make a show of hands. When being truthful or forthcoming, effective leaders tend to use open gestures, showing their palms and wrists, and spreading their hands and arms away from their bodies, as if saying "See, I have nothing to hide." When you think about what the opposite of that—folded arms, hands behind the back, or jammed in pockets—conveys, you see what an easy and effective way this is to establish trust.

Too much really is too much. I've had to learn this the hard way. Genuine enthusiasm and expressing your passion with your body language is great, and I encourage you to express yourself, but be mindful not to cross the line. Too much will be perceived as your trying too hard, so the next time you want to jump up and down in excitement about something, think before you jump. Early in my career, it was perceived as immature. And with the help of a coach, I learned how to manage my dance moves, which in my twenties was what I would do with big news—my very own happy dance. Believe me, I still dance, but only when it's the right time!

Align your words and gestures. Alignment, synergy, and timing with your words and gestures are important in supporting the message. The goal: congruency. You never want your words to be expressing one thing and your gestures the opposite. For example, many people fold their arms across their chests, and this instantly creates a boundary. No matter what your message, crossed arms will *never* help you convey it.

Don't use pacifiers. Many people get nervous when they are going to speak with someone new or during a meeting or presentation and reach for "pacifiers"—pens, paper clips, or rubber bands. When you are speaking with someone and your hands are playing with a pen cap, for example, it will be perceived as insecurity.

Smile! Facial expression is another form of nonverbal communication, and a genuine smile goes a long way. Smiling adds warmth and an aura of confidence. Smiles are also contagious, so as you smile more, others will, too.

Walk tall. Posture is just as important as your mother always said it was. Sit or stand erect if you want to be seen as prepared, enthusiastic, and ready for business. Poor posture sends a message that you are tired or weak. Genius always walks tall. If you have to invest in a posture-correcting brace to help remind you of your posture, do it. It helps.

Watch your figure. How and where you cross your legs says a great deal about how you feel, and too much movement signals nervousness. The preferred positions for any professional are feet flat on the floor or legs crossed at the ankles. The least professional and most offensive position is resting one leg or ankle on top of your other knee. Some call this the "figure four." It can make you look arrogant.

Measure your distance. How close or far you stay from others is crucial if you want to establish good rapport. Standing too close will brand you as pushy, and if you are too far away you will be perceived as standoffish. The goal is to find the happy medium. Most important, do what makes the other person feel comfortable.

You had me at "Hello." A firm handshake, a slight bow, or an air kiss (when appropriate) with any greeting works wonders—as long as you're mindful of the cultural nuances. In America, between Americans, a warm, confident greeting, accompanied by direct eye contact, is always the way to go. When it comes to everyday social and business greetings other rules apply. Do your homework, and get it right when traveling.

Practice, Practice, Practice

This is an aspect of learning to express your genius that I think is monumentally important. You've worked so hard to find your other G-spot. You think you have your genius story just where you want it. But the only way to see how it'll play in Peoria is to practice your story up one side and down the other. Practice it in the mirror, practice it on video, practice it in the car while you're driving. Try it out on random people you've just met, to work the kinks out. Listen for how the rhythms of the story are working, the high points, the segues, the way you wrap it up. You'll know when it works because you'll practically hear a "click."

When I was invited to be a speaker at TEDGlobal 2010 in Oxford, England, I practiced my story for sixty-two hours. I had four minutes to share my idea, and I decided upon my "gifted story" and practiced more for those four minutes than I have ever practiced for any other talk in my life. The result was a near-flawless delivery from my heart and mind, and the outcome was acceptance and celebration from a not-so-easy-to-impress audience. Many of us do not practice the short two- or four-minute stories that we share all day long—but believe me, they're much more effective when you do. Whether on a TED stage or on a subway, I have my themes, vocabulary, and stories edited, practiced, and ready to go. If your intention is to express genius anytime—*every time*—and anywhere, you have to be prepared to do so. I've been blessed with many opportunities throughout my life, and I think it's because I'm prepared when opportunity comes knocking.

PERFECTING YOUR OWN TWO-MINUTE GENIUS STORY

Expressing genius is like writing a book. It features a narrative, is filled with the great themes that clearly speak of you, the hero of the story, and is built with a unique set of words that convey the style and essence of the message and its messenger. You do not have to be a master communicator to get this right. All it takes is dedicating time to writing it, sharing it, editing it, and practicing it. In this era of broadcasting our lives to the world in real time, we really have to be careful not to tell the stories we think people want to hear but the meaningful, authentic ones that matter. You are the author, the composer, the sculptor of your message.

PLAYBOOK

Do the Two-Minute Drill

Put together a story you might tell a person you've just met that will make him or her care about you in no more than two minutes. The story should offer a glimmer of your assets and a sense of who you are. And it should elicit an emotional response, whether it's laughter, empathy, or compassion. Two minutes is all you have. Write it out, practice it with a timer, and practice it on your family. Then try it on a stranger. You'll know right away if it works! You will also benefit from videotaping your two-minute drill with a camcorder or a Flip camera. It will give you ample opportunity to review and evaluate how effective you are and how you can improve both the story itself and the way you deliver it.

PORTRAIT OF A PRACTICAL GENIUS

Magda Yrizarry is the most senior-level Latina at Verizon. She was born and raised by her mother in a housing tenement in a not-so-great part of Brooklyn, New York. Her father died when she was three, which left her mother to raise three young children alone. Although she comes from humble beginnings, she has climbed the corporate ladder in classic American style. But that is not the story she tells about herself. "My personal motto, which I've had all my life, comes from my mother," she says. "When we were kids she drilled this into our heads: 'To whom much is given, much is expected.' We didn't have material wealth, but we were blessed and fortunate and had every opportunity presented to us and with that, came the obligation to pass it on."

Describing how she engages her theme when she speaks, she shared a genuine nugget of truth: "Gina, you can't fake it." As Verizon's chief diversity officer and vice president for talent management, she knows a thing or two about effective communications, and what she has learned about recruiting, retaining, and advancing diverse talent at Verizon is that you really have to offer meaningful experiences and substance. Anything else is of little value. Magda offers many profound observations within her unique vocabulary, which I like to call "Magdaisms," that speak the truth of her but also leverage her authentic genius. When Magda says, "You can't fake it," she's preaching that we must engage from the heart and give the communities within and outside the workplace what they really want—a rich, authentic experience.

She delivers this message and effort through what she calls "CPR": communication, partnership, respect. I have always been impressed with how Magda is consistent with her narrative, her themes, and her unique vocabulary. Her entire life consistency without compromise, and everyone who works or partners with or otherwise experiences her knows exactly what they are going to get—a straight shooter who doesn't waiver in her unique, direct approach to expressing herself.

Another Magdaism I have come to live by is "Be predictable." By predictable she doesn't mean bologna-sandwich-for-lunch-every-single-day predictable; she means you can set your watch by her values and behavior and expectations. To Magda, authenticity and this kind of value-driven consistency go hand in hand, and she is one of the few people I know who has made this particular connection and expresses it so distinctively. This quality has gained her great credibility and access at the highest levels, and she swears by it. "My 'predictability' has gotten me invited to many a decision table," she explains. "My colleagues know I'm going to show up prepared, knowledgeable, and will only participate if I have something meaningful to contribute to the conversation. This gives people confidence in the quality of their experience with me." Just as every sip of Starbucks coffee is consistent from cup to cup to cup, so is every experience with genius-brand Magda.

Magda's other G-spot is the convergence of her classic type-A leadership skills and her passion for enabling change and growth in everyone around her. Whether presenting at a board meeting, serving on a mission to the Dominican Republic, or arranging scholarships for underprivileged children, Magda's authenticity and predictability gain her mind share and loyalty from everyone she works with.

SUMMING UP

- Expressing your genius is about turning that sweet spot where your hard and soft assets meet into the story you tell others. A person without a story is invisible.
- Visual tools can light a spark of understanding of your own genius. Play with those tools.
- Cultivate the art of telling your story. Be both an editor and a listener. Become acquainted with your voice. Get your body into the game. And practice your story until it's as familiar to you as a song on the radio.
- Marry your authentic narrative to the themes of your aspirations and the language of your strongest assets, both soft and hard. Provide illustrations that fascinate and illuminate. Invest the necessary time, energy, and resources in the story you have to tell about your genius.

You know where your genius lives, and you've developed the story and tools that will help you convey your genius to others. You are beginning to understand that genius isn't a part-time commitment; it's a 24/7 proactive, strategic experience, and your full-time job is to grow it in yourself and project it to others while you work, play, listen, dream, sell, negotiate, speak, volunteer, travel, read, present, breathe, sleep, and live!

SURROUND YOURSELF WITH GENIUS

You Are Who You Walk With

If you did an inventory of your relationships—your friends, family, colleagues—what would it say about you? Specifically, are the people in your life an accurate reflection of who you are? Do they share your values, support your passions, and encourage your growth as a human being? Do you see your own joy, curiosity, and energy in them? Have you handpicked them with care, or are they in your life by happenstance?

I almost don't have to say another word here, do I? You're already flipping through the snapshots of your people in your head. Some are 100 percent solid and reflect every good and genius thing about you; others make you scratch your head a little, don't they? How did they fall in with your crew in the first place? Oh, right. There's family—you can't choose them, you get what you get. And there are people you've collected over the years in the workplace—that guy who sat next to you at your first job, the woman who partnered with you on a project.

And your friends? They're your peeps! You can call them anytime, day or night, to laugh, cry, gripe, commiserate. They know your secrets and share your inside jokes.

Well, news for you: None of these is a good enough reason for any of those people—even your family—to hold a place in your life. Here's why.

The people in your life are the cast of characters in your genius story. If the characters don't support the story, what do you have? An incoherent, out-of-balance, unrewarding script, like one of those ridiculous movies that you walk out of at the theater. You are also likely in a situation where you work and work to sustain these relationships but can't quite account for their benefit to you. Look, we all feel a little guilty about the less-than-gratifying relationships that we continue out of emotional laziness or fear of change or wanting to avoid hurting someone's feelings. But if you can see the shimmer of the promise of your genius right before you—and by this moment in your journey, that's right where you should be—you have an obligation to consider whether the people in your life are feeding and supporting your genius or causing you to spend emotional energy and precious time at great cost to your potential.

Don't worry—no one's going to make you throw your friends and family overboard. I'm just going to make you level with yourself about what you've got and make a plan to improve the company you keep.

Shortly after I quit my job to start my own practice, I took a hard look at the people in my life and realized that 95 percent of my personal and professional crew consisted of wonderful, loving people who were content with a life of conformity, security, and safety—which was precisely what I was walking away from. And these people are important to me!

Over the course of my life, they've been there for me and I for them. But I had made this life-changing personal discovery and now saw clearly that most of those folks were not the characters who would populate my genius story. They would never lose their place of importance in my heart, but I had to be truthful with myself about who I needed to be walking with on the revolutionary journey I had just begun.

Feeling quite alone on my risky new exploration of heart and mind, I longed to meet other risk takers, unconventional thinkers, and folks who were already succeeding at a life at the fringes of their organizations and communities, driven not by the acquisition of wealth but by the acquisition of new ideas. I knew I needed to surround myself with people who were exploring their intellectual curiosities with great fervor, and I wanted to spend time with others whose work had become their play. And most important, I knew I needed to forge meaningful relationships with people who were already living nontraditional lives at their genius axis.

So I set out on a quest to surround myself with genius, to populate my life and time with people who were right where I wanted to be, who would stimulate and inspire me, share their wisdom and enthusiasm, and seek the same from me. I had no intention of throwing my people overboard—or "weeding my friendship garden" as one mischievous pal likes to say. I was just going to invite some amazing new people into my boat.

A relationship is a choice, not an accident (no matter how many accidental people there seem to be in your life). I knew that the relationships I wanted to invest in should be both an expression and an extension of my genius. So I made a plan. My plan was based on the idea of curating an experience, as at a museum or another kind of exhibition. A good curator knows how to take a theme or concept and identify and assemble all of the components that will make the experience extraordinary. The best-curated experiences reflect a broad view that ensures an appreciation of the "big picture," as well as a creative perspective that enables intuition, personal experience, and serendipity to come into play.

With that in mind, I developed a list of twenty-five very different people whose stories intrigued me, whose work I had read or read about, whom I was intensely curious about, but whom I didn't know—yet. Fueled by a crazy, nothing-to-lose fearlessness, I began reaching out to these people with a simple request for a conversation. Very much in my own very focused, very dynamic genius zone, I was delighted but not surprised when those people agreed to meet or speak with me. After all, my passion and my purpose were not to be denied! What does surprise me is that more than half of the people on my "genius wish list" are now a part of my life. But that's what you'll discover when you make the effort to make genius connections in your life: genius loves company.

As you shift the balance of the people in your life from "just because" to "on purpose," this is what you have to look forward to: playdates of genius and even trips of genius with people as curious and dynamically motivated as yourself; a life filled with givers versus takers, creators versus destroyers, feeders versus vampires; and days shared with visionaries with real smarts who are committed to changing the game in their own lives and in the lives of others. The transfer of knowledge and insight is best experienced through the lens of others, and finally deciding to surround yourself with nothing shy of amazing is not a wish but a demand that practical geniuses must make of themselves.

Every genius is unique, so the possibilities are endless when considering the kinds of folks you want to begin to fold into your life. I find it helpful to think of the geniuses in my life in three broad categories: the Yodas, the ambassadors, the fat brains, and the tribe. This isn't to pigeonhole anyone in your life, but rather to be sure you're surrounding yourself with the range of geniuses that can really make a difference. I also believe there's an effective process for courting genius that causes you to identify, initiate, seed, and grow the successful relationships you seek.

Warning: if you are thinking "I don't need any new friends" or "I have enough people in my life," you are about to miss the personal paradigm shift of a lifetime. But if you're ready to curate your cast of characters and you're prepared for the extraordinary rewards that will result, let's get to work.

PLAYBOOK

Inventory Your People

Make a thorough list of the people you are currently surrounded by—your family, colleagues, friends, even acquaintances who seem to get a regular amount of your time. Who are those people? What do they care about? Do they add value to your life and to your story? Or do they deplete your genius resources? Put stars next to the names of the folks who feed you. We'll come back to the ones who don't.

YOU ARE WHO YOU WALK WITH

When I set out to surround myself with genius, I first focused on an array of authors, educators, and entrepreneurs who I suspected were living right at the intersection of what they love and where they excel. Your genius wish list may consist of musicians, techies, or innovative policy makers. The idea is to identify the kinds of folks you want in your life and go about building bridges to the meaningful relationships you believe will feed your genius.

For example, one of the first geniuses on my wish list was the amazing Dan Pink. I had read *A Whole New Mind,* and it was one of those books that made the light click on inside me at just the time I needed it, in the early months of my new venture. I e-mailed him and asked for an interview, and to my surprise he said, "Sure, why not?" So I flew to Washington, D.C., drove to a school in Maryland where he was speaking, then interviewed him on a playground after his presentation. Our conversation was everything I'd hoped for and nothing like I'd expected. But it was then I realized that not only was it possible to spend the rest of my life surrounded by genius, it was an imperative. Now I realize that I had aimed straight for the top in reaching out to Dan but the courage it took to ask and secure this "win" from someone whose words inspired me, gave me the confidence to begin to reach out to others who ignited me in one way or another.

I remember thinking to myself on my flight back from D.C., "If Dan Pink could open up his heart and mind to me, maybe others will as well." After that first success, one by one, I went after each person on my list and invited them for what I call "nontransactional practical genius meet-and-greets," where I made it clear that I was looking for nothing more than a conversation, a chance to ask a few questions and be exposed to their thinking. And most agreed to do it. After Dan, I contacted Martha Beck, who kindly gave me an interview backstage at a conference where she was speaking. This exchange was invigorating for both of us and led to her inviting me for a weekend retreat she hosted in Arizona. Next I met up with Eva Longoria for an intimate interview on Latina genius, then bonded with Suze Orman over our shared connection with the ocean.

Though it was fun meeting those mega-brand geniuses, it was most deeply rewarding to meet the practical geniuses like me who are quietly (or not so quietly!) but deliberately designing their lives in nontraditional ways. For example, my tribe now includes the young founders of Summit Series, an entrepreneurial venture comprised of folks who've decided to live, travel, and work together, modern-day nomads moving around every couple of months as they advocate for young entrepreneurs globally. Then there's Lady YaYa, a Turkish mom who decided to go back to school for her master's degree in architecture, balancing motherhood and school in an extraordinary way. Or the amazing Adeline Heymann, a twenty-something financial professional and gifted photographer who specializes in foreclosure prevention at Fannie Mae and also teaches homeless kids about photography. The list goes on and on, including educators, techies, artists, executives, activists, small-business owners, and at-home dads who have humbled me with their unique genius and generosity of spirit.

Thinking back on the many genius meet-and-greets I have had over the last two years, I realize that every single encounter was a lot like a first date, and if there was genius synergy, as was often the case, the result was the start of a genuine friendship. My intention enabled and ignited the connection, and the rest followed.

THE POWER OF GENIUS INTENTION

It is my belief that there are no coincidences in life, just the power of intention. I made my list of twenty-five and used all my resources, creativity, and intuition to make connections with them. Every encounter fed me just as I'd hoped it would, built my confidence, and enabled me to make stronger, more purposeful, more personal connections each time. Today the list has been replaced with a fierce intention to connect with practical geniuses everywhere I go. We find one another on airplanes, at concerts, at dinners, at my son's school, at the library, at TEDx events, in coffee houses, and (of course!) in bars and dance clubs around the globe. They're out there—the people who can teach you, beat your drum with you, encourage and inspire you, make you smarter, and just make you better at who you are.

How do you find them? The same way I do, by moving through the world with an open and receptive mindset, essentially projecting your genius on a frequency that I promise other geniuses are tuned in to, too. It's a kind of shared energy that's a combination of intense curiosity, smart cool hunting, and a natural confidence that is both attractive and accessible. You're also vibing a potential for intelligent camaraderie that the people you might connect with are vibing right back.

For example, I can be standing in the security line at the airport, and without fail, my energy will connect with someone else's, and inevitably a conversation begins. Before long, we are looking for a Starbucks to have a coffee together before our flights. It happens in elevators, too, these harmonious energy exchanges with strangers that lead to two-minute chats and an exchange of contact info to reconnect at another time. Think of these innumerable possible genius connections as energy seeds you are constantly flinging out to the universe that will land and take root exactly where they ought to. Your approach should be purposeful but also genuinely open to anything. When you're in the zone, your genius detector is on all the time and the potential for genius connections is constant and limitless.

Knowing this is true, I move through my day tuned to seek out the genius of others, and when I sense one, instead of letting the opportunity go by, I make a point of introducing myself. Quickly following the introduction, I ask a question: What do you care most about? This is the question that invites the other person to either share his or her authentic story or head for the hills. If the latter happens—which from time to time it does—it's not that that person didn't really have the genius vibe, it's that they he or she wasn't ready for *me*. When I engage with someone, I *really* lead with my passion—and there are times when I can be a little high octane for a perfect stranger! Those who are ready for that first conversation with me, though, dive right in, and the harmony and melody begin to sync up all at once. Some of these exchanges go on for hours; others are quick-deep connections that last all of ten minutes. Asking a meaningful question is a great way to measure people's fluency with and access to their own genius, and those that are living at their other G-spot always respond, share, and join the symphony of the moment.

On the notion of surrounding oneself with genius, Dan Pink explains, "You have to take some risks, and you have to be intentional, and I think even more important than that, you have to be willing, as brutal as it sounds, to sort of tap aside the people who don't fit the bill. People tend to fall into two categories: those who make your life easier and those who make it harder. Those whose presence helps you perform better and those whose presence makes you do worse. I think the best approach is to be one of the people who you want to be around."

Think about this for a second. Are you one of the people you want to be around? Are you putting all your best stuff out there? Are you fearless and generous with your genius? To attract genius, you have to be intelligently, naturally, but purposefully projecting it, telling your story, living out there in your genius zone for all to see.

PLAYBOOK

Your Genius Wish List

Make a list of the people in your scope of learning, curiosity, and passion whose work or expression inspires you. These are people who you read or read about, who get stuck in your head and you find yourself talking like a fan about them or recommending them to others. Include also on your list people in your local sphere whom you don't know but you're curious about or about whom you've heard interesting things. Throw a couple of monster brands in there, too, high-profile folks whose work and message represent a gold standard in your life.

Next to each name, sketch out a strategy for reaching out to them, whether by e-mail or phone call or through an introduction from another person. Be specific in your "ask," which ideally should be a simple, fairly brief conversation by phone or over a cup of coffee. Be clear that you want nothing more than a bit of time to hear about what they're doing, that this is a strictly nontransactional scenario you are proposing. Be resourceful. Arrange to attend a seminar or event where one of your geniuses will be speaking. At the end, introduce yourself and ask for five minutes to ask a couple of questions or to interview that person for your own work. You'll be surprised how accessible people can be when you're modest and specific in your request.

And when you get your moment with them (and you will!), be ready with a smart, sharp script. Like my question "What do you care most about?" or others more specifically connected to your own genius experience, as when I asked Dan Pink about how he approaches curating the people in his life. Be ready to inquire, be ready to share, don't take more time than you asked for, and follow up with your thanks. Then watch your tribe grow.

FILL YOUR LIFE WITH GENIUSES

Once you begin living with the surround-yourself-with genius mindset, there's no limit to the number of extraordinary people who will make their way into your life. I think that they generally fall into three categories: your Yodas, the ones who are rich with experience and will teach you and mentor you on your journey; your ambassadors, the ones who are best at sharing you, connecting you with people you should know, and spreading your ideas and genius assets; your tribe, which is you and the wide-ranging crew of online and real-time people who feed and inspire one another in a magnitude of ways, and your fat brains, those magnificently multidimensional cultural modernists who simply expand your horizons. Some of your people will fall into all of these categories, and they are your all-stars, your go-tos, your A-team. Some you may never meet face-to-face, but you depend on the infusion of smarts or passion or creativity you share regularly through your virtual communication. Wherever they fall on your genius-crew spectrum, they are as important to growing your genius as the air you breathe. Let's have a closer look at who they are.

YOUR YODAS

Throughout my life I have been fortunate to have elders who have schooled me and genuinely had my back throughout my journey. I consider these generous teachers to be Yodas, the wise masters and human compasses who help to tease out our powers, point us to what we're missing, and always elevate our self-awareness. The original big-screen Yoda saved Luke Skywalker from himself, revealed him to himself, and showed him the immense and extraordinary power he had inside him all along. You see why having a Yoda is important to a genius!

I believe that we all need a minimum of two Yodas in our lives. Your Yodas are the coaches, advisers, tutors, and mentors who will answer the uncomfortable questions, who offer unconditional support, fierce loyalty, and unfailingly objective feedback. They are the intellectuals, teachers, nurturers, change agents, and wise angels in your life.

Someone once asked me to explain the value of a Yoda, and I replied, "The Yoda teaches you what no one else had the courage or capacity to teach you about yourself." Lessons like "Gina, when you reject drama in your life, it is only then that life becomes poetic." Lessons like "Anything is possible for you when you act *as if.*" And truths such as "Never, ever take no for an answer; debate, negotiate, wheedle, and cajole, and you will change a no into a yes."

These are probably good lessons for anyone, but they particularly suited my nature, personality, and experience. Convincing me of the truth of this wisdom required the Yoda to know me well, which is another key characteristic of your Yodas. My aunt Maria was my first Yoda, someone who watched me and knew how to read me and motivate me; most of all, she provided an example of how to conduct myself that has never left me.

Growing up as an only child without the influence of or guidance from siblings was sometimes difficult. My aunt filled that gap and taught me what she knew I needed to know. She taught me how to dance the hustle, how to jump a fence without ripping my clothes, how to appreciate classical music, and how to pick the best pickles from a barrel at the Delancey Street market. She taught me how to roller-skate, how to cross between subway cars, and—this was the tops—how to ride on the handlebars of a ten-speed bike while she pedaled us along the East River. In other words, she taught me how to take risks, how to fly.

My aunt Maria was always filled with beautiful contradictions, which introduced me to the notion of just accepting everything around you without conforming to everything around you. She grew up in one of the worst public housing projects in New York City at the time and ended up at New York University majoring in classical music, playing concert flute, and later going on to law school. Her success demonstrated all that was possible, and her ability to overcome adversity was a testament to what determination can accomplish. And she made sure I discovered those same things about myself. She is still my Yoda, but what I love best about our relationship is that today I'm her Yoda, too. Now, we mentor each other.

Mentor was a figure from Greek mythology, a friend of Odysseus who was left to tend to and teach Odysseus's son, Telemachus, when Odysseus left for the Trojan War. Hence there is a particular element of trust and intimacy to the notion of a mentor. You must be able to put yourself in your mentors' hands, knowing that they will share their wisdom, help guide your path, and encourage you to think ahead to your future. The dynamic between mentor and protégé can be forged and played out in different ways, of course, depending on how and why you find yourself in the relationship in the first place. Following are three familiar scenarios.

The Institutional Yoda

Many of today's mentor/protégé relationships are formal relationships born within organizations, someone having discovered, I suppose, how valuable a professional development tool this can be! Advancement has become nearly impossible without the benefit of a mentor in the workplace. In many organizations, it is a requirement of mentors to engage in such a relationship with a more junior employee, just as it is a requirement of employees to engage with a mentor. The success of these institutional relationships is entirely based on the commitment of the mentor and the protégé. With the opportunity to scope out the people who might be effective mentors before engaging with one, you might end up with a mentor who has just the right instinct and experience to help you flourish. If you are assigned to a mentor, though, without the chance to explore the prospects for the relationship, it's like getting picked for the dodgeball team in junior high gym class, just the luck of the draw. Don't forget to duck.

Chemistry is key, but so is motivation. In other words, given your intention of surrounding yourself with people who feed and encourage your genius, there's a lot you can make happen just by the power of your purpose. While working toward my master's in public administration as a National Urban Fellow in New York City, I was given a mentorship assignment to work as the "special assistant" to Sheila Wellington, who was at that time the president of Catalyst, a leading nonprofit organization committed to expanding opportunities for women in business. At the beginning I wasn't sure what my role in this relationship would entail, but I quickly learned it meant working on whatever Sheila thought would be "good for me."

I was prepared to extract every ounce of value from the experience, but I was not prepared for Sheila's incredible commitment to my growth and education. She allowed me to shadow her the entire time I worked with her, never leaving me out of any aspect of her day. That meant I was able to watch and learn from her experience as a powerful woman on a mission to help educate CEOs about the imperative of advancing female talent. After I completed my master's degree, Sheila hired me to work on the first-ever Women of Color in Corporate Management study.

Looking back, I realize that Sheila looked straight to my potential and focused on teaching me some critical things no one had taught me before. This included everything from the art of listening to the power of keeping your word to professional etiquette and how to write a killer thank-you note. Sheila is a master communicator and in many respects was one of my first editorial teachers. I will admit that sometimes I had to learn the hard way, but it was worth the pain I sometimes experienced behind closed doors after one of her "reality checks" with me.

Sheila, a classic, old-school straight shooter, expressed her commitment to my potential by being persistently patient and unfailingly honest with me as I was learning. For example, I remember once she recommended I write a thank-you note to one of the women I had interviewed for the Women of Color in Corporate Management study, and when I submitted my first draft to Sheila for her feedback she handed it back to me and said to try again. I ended up rewriting that thank-you note fourteen times, every time getting a bit closer but not quite there. Sheila could easily have said, "Never mind, I'll write it for you," but instead she coached me through every draft until I got it. Fifteen years later, I still handwrite all my thank-you notes, and every time I remember exactly what Sheila taught me about the precise art of saying "thank you."

Now, you might be wondering what Sheila has gained from this fifteen-year relationship. The benefit to her, I think, has been the value of mutual, intelligent honesty. Just as Sheila has been candid with me, I have always been straightforward and open with her. Many times while we worked together, I would give her my honest opinion when others didn't dare to. Another benefit has been the lively and unexpected mutual learning. For example, Sheila introduced me to the Victorian novelist Anthony Trollope; I taught her how to use virtual currency.

Too many of us assume that the Yodas in our lives "know everything," but in my experience, they are as grateful as I am when someone takes the time to channel new information, insight, and trends their way. Whether it's a link to an article I read, a book I think she would like, or just sharing my life lessons as an entrepreneur with her, Sheila always appreciates the depth of our conversations and diverse range of topics and perspective that I bring to the table.

Today Sheila sits on the board of the New York Women's Foundation and is a professor of women's corporate leadership at the Stern Business School at NYU, and we still have a strong relationship. In fact, she is my rock. Whenever I am facing a big life decision, I always consult with Sheila first. "Sheila, I think I want to move to Miami, what do you think?" "Sheila, I think I want to quit my job to write a book, what do you think?" "Sheila, I think I'm ready for motherhood, what do you think?" When I'm at one of these junctures, the ritual is to meet her at the Century Club in New York City and commune from the heart.

The Surrogate-Parent Yoda

There is a kind of informal mentorship relationship that is more oriented toward nurturing than process or toward a specific objective. My aunt Maria certainly falls into this category. Your relationship with this Yoda often offers the best of a kind of parent-child relationship, because it's based on care and closeness but lacks some of the traditional issues with which true parent-child relationships can be fraught. The female mentors who adopted me as their "daughter" were always pushing me, protecting me, dressing me, grooming me, and plenty of times gently scolding me. Those kinds of Yodas lead with the maternal/paternal aspect of their natures and really don't know any other way. They also tend to be "lifers," who stay with their protégés over the course of a lifetime. It is a great blessing to be adopted by such a Yoda.

Over the years I've been blessed with several surrogate-parent Yodas, and each of them has been instrumental in exposing me to the world beyond the borders of the United States. In my junior year as a literature and rhetoric major at Binghamton University, I dreamed of studying abroad but didn't have the resources to do it. It was then that I was "adopted" by an amazing professor, Dr. Carole Boyce Davies, who helped me secure the funding to participate in the English Department's study-abroad program. Dr. Davies taught abroad that year and basically took me with her, and it was truly an act of love. I studied English literature at Regents College in London for a year and backpacked throughout Europe with other students. I can't tell you how unlikely it was that this Puerto Rican kid from New York City would have this experience.

Four years later I was adopted once again by two community leaders, Alice Cardona and Yolanda Sanchez, who had been impressed by my success organizing a Puerto Rican youth conference called "Muevete," and invited me to travel with them to China for the NGO Fourth World Conference on Women in 1995. I received a scholarship from the United Nations to do just that and traveled around China for a month with other female delegates from the United States.

Thinking back on all the surrogate-parent Yodas I have had, I realize that they were all advocates, extreme nurturers, and, in my case, frequently overlapped with the youth and community organizing efforts I was involved in during my twenties. In my experience, the public sector and NGO world are full of these kinds of mentors. If you lead with your heart, impress them with your energy, and have a positive measureable impact, those folks will pass it forward and make things happen for you.

Note that you are never too old to enjoy the support of a

surrogate-parent Yoda. I have found as I get older that for the overextended professional, the nurturing aspect of this kind of relationship is especially rewarding. While other Yodas provide logical, left-brain kind of support in your life, surrogate parents tend to focus on the protégé's entire life experience and context rather than one slice of it.

The Yoda-for-Hire

During my last year with PR Newswire, I was offered a stretch assignment, and as part of my compensation for this additional work, I negotiated for an executive coach. Several friends at other companies were working with executive coaches, and I was curious to see and experience what a "paid mentor" would be like for me, someone who's a big sponge and constant learner. The most interesting revelation was that I found myself working extra hard at achieving outcomes in this relationship because of the financial investment that was made for the service. It's the same thing that happens when you pay for a personal trainer or a therapist—you do the work because you want your money's worth.

Now, not all executive coaches are the same. They have different techniques and personalities, and, as with your trainer or therapist, before you engage in a relationship like this, you want to hear from others that the person is great to work with! You want to know exactly what the benefits and outcomes of this relationship will be because you're paying for it. But that's the best reason in the world to seek a Yoda-for-hire, when you have a particular objective that someone with a particular skill can help you achieve.

For example, after my unfortunate experience with the shingles, I knew I wanted an executive coach who was an expert in stress management as well as leadership. I also knew I wanted someone with a bit of edge, and after interviewing four coaches I ended up choosing Angela Love, an expert in neuroleadership who taught me—among many other things—how to meditate with nonachievement in mind.

Angela got me to begin scratching at my genius potential by teaching me how to exercise unseen "leadership muscles" while meditating. This practice resulted in better patience and quiet confidence and, most important, taught me courage, which eventually helped me take the leap to start my own practice. Angela was a great coach, and my experience with her taught me the real power of Yodas-for-hire.

There's nothing wrong with "paying for it" if you know that this Yoda will play a role in feeding and growing your genius. But you have to base the work on your genius needs, define the objective, and measure the outcome. That's very different from the more organic nature of an institutional mentor or a surrogate-parent relationship. For whatever reasons they arise, those are relationships that have more natural rhythms and usually less precisely defined objectives. Their common denominator, though, of course, is that all these Yodas are operating from their own genius zone, at the place of their greatest power, and can inspire, motivate, and support *your* genius.

PLAYBOOK

Got Yoda?

This is an inventory of what you've already got. Comb through your lifetime experience and identify any individual who played Yoda to your Skywalker. It can be a kindergarten teacher, a sports coach, a relative, colleague, manager, or friend. What qualities defined those relationships, and what qualities did those people possess that made them such effective mentors? Are any of them still in your life? If so, are you caring for the relationship, or is it on autopilot? If not, which of those relationships would be a good model for a new relationship you might pursue?

The Ask

If your dance card is already full of more Yodas than you can handle, good for you. More likely, though, you're realizing that you're way low in the mentor department. You can see how helpful it would be to have that rudder, that mirror, that swift kick in the pants when you need it most. People come into and out of your life in these roles, and it's common to wake up one day and realize that you've been flying solo a little too long.

If you have access to a formal mentorship program in your workplace or another organization, such as a church or community group, get hooked up with it. You may or may not find a genius in the mix with whom you want to ally yourself, but it's more likely you'll find one if you're actively looking, right?

If you had a positive mentor relationship that you've allowed to fall dormant, think about reactivating it. There are all kinds of reasons your relationship may have lapsed, but if it was strong and positive for both of you, there's a very good chance that that Yoda will be delighted to hear from you and for the chance to reengage.

Finally, you can start from scratch, as any resourceful genius would do. Think hard about the people you've been exposed to in your personal life and your work. Is there someone you've admired but have never had the opportunity to engage with? Is there a wise genius you once worked or played with whom you could now enlist as a Yoda? Or is it time to get out your wallet and get a professional Yoda involved in your progress?

In any of these instances, the trick is how to ask. You can't just knock on someone's door and say, "Will you be my Yoda?" Not cool. But it is simpler than it seems. You can be direct, especially in a formal situation in the workplace. You can also informally sidle up to someone, get to know him or her, feel him or her out, and, if you feel a click, ask if he or she has the time and inclination to work with you. Or you can go total stealth by developing a relationship with the intention of making the person your Yoda but never saying a word about it until you're there! It's kind of a Lucy Ricardo move, but sometimes just planting the seed and quietly watching it grow is enough.

The most important thing is to stick to your genius agenda. Once the relationship with a Yoda begins, be sure to share your genius learning goals. It's a complete waste of time if you don't say out loud what you're working toward. It can be a hard-asset goal, such as expanding your expertise in a particular area, or it can be a soft-asset goal, such as developing a particular creative outlet. Being specific makes the learning richer, more efficient, and more focused. You can and should pursue multiple goals, of course, but it has been my experience that the best way to access their genius is to focus on one of their strengths.

For example, in my own life I have focused on specific learning goals with each of my Yodas, most recently ranging from entrepreneurial learning goals to writing goals to developing my emotional intelligence. No matter what the relationship, though, I always have a learning goal in mind and, in my own way, ensure that the other person is learning, too.

A Note About the Role of the Protégé

As a protégé, your job is to be open, flexible, available, and 100 percent present in the relationship. When you give yourself up to the process and commit to the trust required for its success, powerful bonding happens. You're invested together in the success of the relationship, and your mutual access to each other's energy, curiosity, and intelligence is a critical motivator for both of you. In other words, it's not all about you. So if you really want it to work for you, you have to give as much as you get. You're certainly the student in this dynamic, but that doesn't mean your Yoda won't grow his or her own genius as a result of engaging with you—that is, if you're really putting it out there. That will be the moment your relationship truly puts down some roots, when the mutual rhythm of giving and receiving goes both ways.

A good mentor will always try to help you "sharpen the saw," as Steven Covey would say. The trick is to be the best student you can be within the context of that relationship. In playing the student role, it's natural to aspire to please our teachers, seeking praise and acknowledgment from them. But sometimes the best kind of learning is experienced not in the praise but in the difficult feedback every good Yoda will share at some point in your relationship. You have to be built not just to withstand constructive criticism but to do everything you can with it to grow your genius. Although the frank feedback from your Yoda is always rooted in what's best for you, the experience of hearing the things we sometimes don't want to hear is often not easy for the protégé. Yet some of the most important growth I have experienced in my life was the result of relationships with mentors who didn't censor themselves and were very direct about what I needed to work on, regardless of what my emotional response might be. Your ego may be bruised during the process, but your strengths will grow stronger and your weaknesses weaker. Some might call this "tough love," but I prefer to call it "responsible education." All mentors should hold their protégés to nothing shy of a standard of excellence.

As I look back on these sometimes rough-and-tumble reality checks, the only way I can describe the outcome is a kind of euphoria. With my editor, Karen, for example, sometimes after hanging up the phone or putting down a handwritten letter from her, I'll be driving or walking somewhere and I begin to feel a bit taller, smarter, wiser, and, most important, humbled and grateful for the gift of strong, insightful guidance that lets me see my work or thinking in a different way. This is the big home run, when someone who knows you and cares about your success can help smooth your path in some way or, if necessary, get out of your own way.

Understand that being able to own the fact that they played an instrumental role in your success is a huge turn-on for good mentors. Like papas, they see a bit of the DNA of their own genius now running through you, which is affirming and gratifying, to say the least. When you succeed, they succeed. The opposite of success in these relationships is mediocrity, because this is an unacceptable reflection on themselves. This is a unique characteristic of this relationship, that each of you is a kind of reflection of each other. It's part of what makes the relationship intensely personal but also potentially extremely powerful.

Besides being a "good student," it is your responsibility as a protégé to keep the attention and maintain the attraction of the mentor by offering "value adds." For me this means sharing advice with them on their own projects or challenges. It means being available as a resource to them, volunteering my talents and skills for their efforts, whether writing for them, hooking them up with someone who can be useful to them, or keeping them current, timely, and relevant. This boils down to paying attention and taking initiative in the relationship, even though the assumed focus is on you, the protégé.

Finally, do right by your Yodas. Be profusely, demonstratively grateful, acknowledge them both privately and publicly, and loop them into your genius network. You are genius assets to each other, after all, and when one of you grows, you both grow.

YOUR AMBASSADORS

In the same way that countries use ambassadors to communicate and spread their agenda, the practical genius relies on ambassadors to be passionate, resourceful connectors who help create opportunities for growth, extending the reach of their message and helping to seed new meaningful genius relationships for them around the globe. These are a unique breed of people; they are the believers, the loyalists, your passionate promoters. They get excited about your genius and are the first to talk you up to someone they "think you should know." This is one of the primary roles ambassadors play in the life of a practical genius; they have strong networks and a geniune belief in the value of putting smart, dynamic people together just for the good of the universe. They're quick, intuitive, 100 percent generous, and 100 percent nontransactional. They are in your life because they believe in your genius, and they are as eager to share you with others as they are to engage with you themselves.

I first considered the notion of ambassadors while going through Keith Ferrazzi's Relationship Masters Academy (RMA), where we explored techniques in building what Keith calls "lifeline ambassador relationships." According to Keith, these are intimate friendships, people with "refrigerator rights" who have agreed to support each other's success. These are people who have chosen to be accountable in helping you achieve your goals.

My experience with ambassadors is more emotional. Unlike your Yodas, who may be available to you only once a month or even quarterly, your ambassadors are there for you day in and day out, whether sitting two doors down from you in your workplace or at a conference on another continent. In fact, proximity to and face time with your ambassadors aren't nearly as important as a deep sympathy, a mutual admiration that makes you want to be backup bands for each other 24/7. The ambassador also has a natural gift for connecting people, a sixth sense for relationships where there might be genius synergy or entrepreneurial opportunity. Ambassadors seem to see the world through different eyes, always scanning the human horizon looking for potential sparks and other kinds of combustion they can instigate.

Ambassadors of the Heart and Mind

Like every genius, the ambassador operates with a heartfelt passion and a keen intelligence and intuition. My friend Katina is a classic ambassador. She is a comrade, a champion, and a "keep it real" kind of person who is the definition of unconditional support and generosity. Katina has an incredible eye for genius; in the last year alone she made over sixty-five introductions on my behalf, a few of whom went straight to the top of my core crew of practical geniuses. I consider her to be my greatest talent scout, and she has helped to expand my genius circle and grow my business more than any consultant or venture capitalist ever could. As a one-woman show, you can see how I would especially benefit from her efforts. She is such a good ambassador that some have mistaken her as my public relations agent, which always makes us laugh.

Perhaps the gold standard of genius ambassadors is the incredible Sunny Bates. For thirty years she has used her knowledge and intuition to create inspired marriages between ideas and capital, between creativity and sponsorship, between genius and its audience. Sunny has the unique ability to project and attract genius at the same time. As a result, she has effortlessly built a vast personal network and carries it with her wherever she goes. She is a tireless ambassador for her network, constantly feeding it and enabling strategic connections that benefit the individuals while strengthening the whole. As a master connector, her clear objective is to help others accomplish their goals. And it isn't selflessness that motivates her but a kind of ambition she feels on behalf of the people she connects.

I think that's the key to understanding what makes a killer ambassador. For both Katina and Sunny Bates, it's a fierce energy focused on the people they believe in—so you see why it's so important to have an ambassador or two surrounding and supporting your genius. Sunny emphasizes the importance of what she calls "intellectual honesty." The relationships she enables are only as good as the truth each represents and the integrity each brings to the relationship. One smart, honest relationship leads to another and another, and before long you have a network of geniuses who are building one another up, enabling one another's success, helping one another grow.

It doesn't matter where in the world they are, your ambassadors are thinking of you in a constant loop, sending you genius vibes of support, ideas, connections, and sometimes even some nice chocolate! You don't, however, get to shop for your ambassadors the way you do for your Yodas or the rest of your tribe. That's because so much of the relationship with your ambassadors is based on a kind of kismet, a love at first sight, a true love forever. In other words, there's an organic kind of passion to it that you can't manufacture. That said, I can tell you that the secret of cultivating kick-ass ambassadors is to be one yourself.

To be an ambassador, you have to operate in a constant state of generosity, honesty, and enthusiasm for the people you believe in. It's a give-give-give situation that on the surface sounds like a lot of work, but the fact is that it's the fuel that runs the engine of genius. I'm not kidding. You see genius in someone else, you do everything you can to help that person realize and activate that genius. You admire someone's work, you make sure everyone you know knows about it. Be a shameless fan, a wizard of word of mouth, a constant peddler of other people's genius. This is not a you-scratch-my-back-I'll-scratch-yours kind of thing; it's a 100 percent authentic and purposeful approach to surrounding yourself with genius by pimping the hell out of someone else's genius. How does that help you? You promote their genius, your genius shines. Oh, and you'll find yourself with more ambassadors than you know what to do with. And you can take that to the bank.

PLAYBOOK

Be an Ambassador

Choose someone in your purview on whom to practice being an ambassador. It can be someone you know well, someone you know slightly, or someone you don't know at all. It only has to be someone in whom you see the spark of genius, the buzz of proof that he or she is operating right where the head and heart connect. Once you've chosen your mark, develop a strategy for promoting and representing that person's genius to the world. Reach out to that person, tell him or her you're a believer, and ask how you can help. Reach out to others you think would appreciate this genius. Make calls, make introductions, send links, and connect the dots across the social media to spread that person across your networks. Make that person's exposure and success your priority, and you will immediately see how powerful an ambassador can be. The beauty of this process is that it doesn't take long to see results.

YOUR TRIBE

Your tribe represents the leaves on your tree, the people in your life who give it color and texture, movement and change. Your Yodas and ambassadors are part of your genius tribe, to be sure, but together with a vast complex of folks with innumerable skills, passions, and values that challenge and complement your own. One big distinction is that you know your Yodas and the ambassadors well but you can go a whole lifetime without actually meeting some of the people in your larger genius tribe. The other distinction is that your Yodas and ambassadors tend to be constants—the anchors, if you will, of your genius tribe. The rest of your tribe can be changing all the time, coming and going, bringing new faces, new ideas, new events, new content, fresh blood, and fresh energy to your day-to-day life. This pulsing organism is comprised of friends and strangers, each chosen as carefully as the other and never with an emphasis on quantity over quality. I don't want 100,000 nameless, meaningless followers; I want 100 eclectic geniuses committed to their own experience and therefore improving mine.

As I travel around the virtual world in search of what I like to call "tell me something I don't already know" moments, I am always surprised and delighted by who I am able meet online and eventually fold into my tribe. I have found that the farther out at the fringes I explore, the more original and interesting the people are. And the more original and interesting the people you stir into your stew, the higher the quality of your tribe. Granted, you have to be willing to invest the time in skipping around online, following trails of intriguing clues and signs of genius life in the universe. On any given day, I will linger on a foodie site where molecular gastronomy chefs gather, check in with my preferred news source, globalvoicesonline.org, which has more than three hundred bloggers and translators who pull together reports from citizen media around the world, and poke around in the experience labs at Business Innovation Factory.

Sometimes I make contact with the geniuses I discover online to ask to know more about what they're doing or test the potential of a relationship. Other times, I pull them into my tribe just by reading them, following them, staying aware of what they're doing. In this case, it's my curiosity and interest in their work and content that connects us, though I tout the "invisible" members of my tribe as much as those who inhabit my real-time life. It doesn't matter if I find you standing next to me in line at the cleaner's, on an index card tacked to a bulletin board at the library, or you're an anonymous deep-space star in the farthest reaches of the online universe—it's about the sharing, the spreading, the absorbing and growing, nudging one another along on our genius journeys. Today, for example, I'm following a yacht manufacturer, a scientist, a group of astronauts, a break dancer, and a Zen master. The greater the global mix, the greater the global learning.

PLAYBOOK

Grow Your Invisible Tribe

If you don't already have a thriving, intensely rewarding relationship with an online tribe, it's time to get started! To begin, look for one person who is leading the way in a particular industry or area of expertise that excites you or about which you want to know more. Look for another who is strictly a creative, the kind of personality who is there just to express and inspire, just to be the muse. Then identify another who is entirely off the beaten path, a voice or message from another planet who will add color, discomfort, or just a bunch of question marks to your thinking.

Follow them online for a couple of weeks or a month. In each case, follow the threads and links those folks point you to, exposing yourself to *their* interests and influences and muses. After this trial period, keep anyone in this group who has expanded your horizons, then turn the page, identify a new test crew, and repeat the process. Share your discoveries with your existing tribe, and get them to share theirs with you. Over time, you'll feel your perspective stretching, your brain growing, and you'll have answers to questions you would have never known to ask. It's fun.

Your Real-World Tribe

If you had a party and invited all of the flesh-and-blood people in your tribe, who would they be? How many geniuses would be milling around, feeding and snacking on one another's genius? I'm not talking about just the people in your power contacts list; I'm talking about the whole range of people with whom you choose to align yourself—your neighbors, the chef from that tapas restaurant you love, the parents from your kid's school, the chick who runs your favorite flower shop. These, too, are characters in your genius story. Have you chosen them carefully because your tastes and talents and values sync up, or are you random travelers who are thrown together by proximity and circumstance?

You don't need any more random people in your life. You need people you believe in and who believe in you. Going back to where this whole conversation started, every relationship is a choice. You can make a choice that feeds your genius, or you can make one that doesn't get you anywhere or, worse, makes you move backward.

When you decide to surround yourself with genius, it all matters—who you spend time with, do business with, play with, even worship with. Your tribe should always consist of the best out there as measured against your own values, passions, and strengths. From the block you choose to live on to the small business you decide to support, both the tribe *and* the village matter to the practical genius.

THE FAT BRAINS

It is my opinion that every practical genius needs some percentage of their tribe to be at least half their age. I consider these young advisers, whom I call "fat brains," to be the next wave of global mentors for business leaders, entrepreneurs, executives, and game changers. Take it from me, having a Millennial as an adviser shifts the paradigm and transforms the way you think of your life and work in the day to day and the long term.

The reverse dynamic, in which the junior mentors the senior, upends your traditional approach to learning. A Millennial's digital fluency, gamer's problem-solving skills, and scrappy creative resourcefulness can change your DNA, making you more nimble, adaptive, and more comprehensively exposed to the broadest spectrum of cultural influences.

Over half of the global population is under the age of thirty. And unless you're under thirty yourself, I'll bet you only a small fraction of your tribe, if any, comes from this demographic. What does that tell you? It tells me we're missing a huge opportunity to dance with these worldly cultural modernists who were raised on a diet of bits and memes and threads of contemporary thinking. They invented the tools, hacked the tools, adapted the tools, turned the tools into toys and the toys into the tools that drive modern life. They are art and information junkies who live seamlessly in multiple worlds and feed off innovation, social change, openness, and transparency. How's that for a reason to get some of these fat brains into your life *right now*?

When you know what you don't know, the fat brain can fill the knowledge gap instantly and with urgency. Sunny Bates, who is a big believer in having young mentors, says, "When you decide to surround yourself with much younger people, you are deciding to look at the world in a different way. For example, they see the online persona, the offline persona, the physical world, and the virtual world not as different spaces but just as one world, seamlessly integrated. There's nothing in a baby boomer's past that could have prepared us for that, and so we are continuously smacked over the head with 'Oh my God, that will never work' followed by 'Wow, that works!' and finally 'It's just insane how much this is working!' That's why they're our best guides, particularly for the future."

I am so hooked on the young fat brains in my life who advise me on everything from writing to identifying new trends that I've created a little Fat Brains Advisory Board. The criteria for joining this exclusive group? You have to be under thirty, know a whole bunch about a subject area in which I am deficient, and be a trailblazer in your own right. Some members of my board include Atalia Aron, my in-house scientist; Julian Amaro, my video and film expert; and Dan Lack, my small-business adviser. They are my personal mentors, and I am their protégée. Together we share, bond, and support one another and prove how magic can happen when you shift the paradigm.

Dan explains the value of this age-reversed mentorship as follows: "We're at two totally different points in our life right now, yet we share similar passions and interests and I am able to bring a different perspective to your experience that sometimes helps you see things in a different light." Dan has been out of college only three years, but in that short time he has created the Meeting of the Big Minds, which is a four-day ideation retreat at his family's ranch in Texas. The meeting brings together his most innovative friends from across the country to connect and share ideas. I attended two of Dan's retreats, and it was there that I became convinced that I needed this breed of young experts and innovators in my tribe—the more the better!

Now you see how crowded your genius life can be, with amazing supporters, sounding boards, instigators, and inspirers. When you're running on all cylinders, it should feel like constant waves of connection and energy that go back and forth between you and your whole tribe. You know what kinds of geniuses you want in your life; now let's talk about how to court them.

RULES OF ENGAGEMENT

There are definitely techniques that work and don't work when it comes to courting genius. I have three simple rules that keep me on the straight and narrow of authenticity, honesty, and transparency when I'm engaging with potential recruits for my tribe.

1. No one-night stands.

When building your tribe, your intention should always be to cultivate sustained, meaningful relationships. Although people come and go in our lives, the world is getting smaller and smaller and the six degrees of separation/goes around comes around truisms are more relevant than ever. So when you begin to engage with people you may want to fold into your life, seek out only as many as you have the bandwith to follow through with. Some people are capable only of one-night stands, which are great interactions during the first meeting followed up with . . . nothing. People don't commit to that when dating, and they don't like it much in the rest of their lives, either. So your reach and sweep for geniuses should be broad, but only as broad as you can responsibly and effectively manage to build upon after a first engagement. Scattering a bunch of seeds and not watering or weeding them is a waste.

2. Skip the ten thousand followers for ten true believers.

Cultivating a corps of geniuses also requires that you show discretion in where you place your efforts. Think about your Twitter followers. Do they participate in the conversation, or are they quiet observers, lurking and feeding but not contributing? There's a big difference between a faceless mass of "friends" and "followers" and a band of devoted, engaged believers in you. Ten true believers will spread your message and build momentum around your genius faster and with far more impact than ten thousand passive followers who may or may not even understand your genius, never mind care about it. Better to play with ten amazing people than pander to ten thousand morons. Sorry, it's true.

3. No transactional behavior allowed.

Never, ever initiate a relationship with the intention of "getting something" from that person. Nontransactional behavior looks like this: you share your story, find a connection, and explore the mutual genius potential of your relationship. That's it. You're not selling anything. Transactional behavior looks like this: You meet an amazing person who would be a tremendous addition to your tribe. She's also some-one you could do business with. You choose the prospect over the person and leverage the positive connection you've made with her in order to make a sale. This is a ridiculous, shortsighted trade-off, throwing the real potential asset of the relationship out for the more immediate financial gain you may or may not realize from it. Trust me, if you lead with your genius intention and connect with the people who can really help you reach your potential, all the profit in the world will follow. Doing business with geniuses is fine, but not until long after you are genuinely invested in and care for each other.

Now what? How do we actually start the courtship process with the geniuses we want in our life?

Start with intimacy. Don't beat around the bush. Go straight into emo-tional intimacy mode with them to telegraph your openness and acces-sibility. In late 2001, single and curious about all the talk about "speed dating," I attended an event where participants were organized to spend six minutes with one person, then move on to the next. Playing it safe, most of the guys across the table from me shared the typical data points (birthplace, college, occupation, etc.). That kind of talk isn't very scintil-lating over the course of a real date, so I'm not sure why any of them thought it would close the deal in six minutes! Then one guy, Stephen, sat across from me, and instead of talking about himself, asked me where I was from, and when I told him New York City, with real concern, he asked how I had been affected by the terrorist attacks on 9/11. The six-minute conversation turned out to be an extraordinary deep dive in which Stephen explained that he had lost both his parents as a teenager and had come to believe that you can't manage destiny. He skipped the small talk and established a genuine intimacy that absolutely got my attention. Two years later, Stephen and I were married. Rather than picking off the leaves of the artichoke layer by layer, go straight for the heart.

Use your stories as your currency, no matter who you are talking to. This is especially true when meeting people of great wealth or power. Instead of feeling intimidated or hung up by class disparity, your stories put you on an eye-to-eye, toe-to-toe footing that opens the doors of connection every single time.

Share the experience with your partner. Many of us meet amazing new people and keep them all to ourselves, neglecting to bring our partners along on the relationship-building journey. It's easy to grow apart from your partner when you don't include him or her in your growth experiences.

Finally, remember that there's a shelf life to that initial buzz of connection you feel with a fellow genius. I make a point of following up with a call or an e-mail immediately and attempt to have lunch or dinner with that person within two weeks of meeting. I also quickly try to find a way to connect that person with someone else in my tribe who can help solve a problem or who I think would be a great genius fit, chemistrywise. I also make a point of making global connections between my new friends and my established tribe. Your new friend is traveling to Japan for the first time? Hook her up with your former colleague who's now working in Tokyo. These are little efforts that have large rewards. But if you don't make them quickly, you will discover that the initial spark between you may already be extinguished.

NOW THAT YOU'RE DATING

Once you feel the engine of your new relationship humming, nudge it along by getting to know what drives the other people and what their passions are. Follow them online in the social media, read what they're blogging about, ask questions. This is when you begin to discover the places and spaces you have in common, where you can begin to add value to each other's lives.

Begin a pattern of outreach, starting with a handwritten note. I find this to be one of the most important gestures to establish intimacy, to make the terms of your relationship personal. E-mail is great; so are phone calls and face time. But a thoughtful letter written in your own hand is like a touch on the shoulder, a brush of the cheek. It matters a lot.

Almost as important as meaningful communication is generous sharing. This is a *mi casa es su casa* thing. Make introductions with abandon; share your assets, share your tribe. Be bold in your sharing; just be clear that every connection you enable, every circle you expand, is nontrasactional.

The most important thing you can do to build and sustain a new relationship is to add value to the person's life. Be there, share, invest in that genius's success. There's been a lot of talk lately about "relationship management" and tools you can use to automate the upkeep of your relationships. I'm a little more organic than that. As a visual person, I find that keeping a photo or another reminder of the essence of each of my geniuses in my sight is the most effective way to keep them at the front of my mind and constantly brainstorming about how to support and connect them with others.

In the end, you are the designer of each of these relationships. It is up to you to apply your unique style to seeding, feeding, and sustaining them. Be creative, strategic, even provocative. Be a champion of the others' passions and causes; be an always-accessible, entirely generous resource. To serve another person is to help him or her grow, and there is no better way to ensure that you are surrounded by exactly the people who care about *your* success and are there to help *you* grow.

Curate Your Group Experiences

I am as big a believer in the power of extraordinary group experiences as I am of experiences based on individual relationships. A truly original group experience can change you, expanding your understanding of yourself in the world. Contrary to the popular perception of conferences and other group events as opportunities to "network," I believe that the successful group experience is about how it personally impacts each individual, not how it inflates their Rolodexes. Whether it's an intimate dinner party, an off-site work session, or an international conference for change agents, the key to ensuring that transformative impact on the individual is to curate very purposefully the participants in the event.

Be a People Collector

Cathy Leff, the director of the Wolfsonian-FIU museum in Miami, emphasizes the importance of being a "people collector." What she means by this is to be deliberate in assembling a wide array of multigenerational, multidisciplinary, culturally diverse minds. I worked with Cathy to put on the first TEDxMIA, a program celebrating local geniuses in Miami. Created in the spirit of TED.com's mission—"ideas worth spreading"—TEDx programs are designed to give communities, organizations, and individuals the opportunity to stimulate dialogue through TED-like experiences at the local level. TEDx events are fully planned and coordinated independently on a community-by-community basis and are a tremendous example of the power of strategically curating your group experience.

When I decided to launch TEDxMIA, I joined more than 1,800 plus curators in ninety-six countries worldwide who have put on more than 1,900 events in more than forty languages. TEDxers, as we call ourselves, are forging genius variations on the group experience around the globe. Chris Anderson, the curator of the TED conferences and TED.com, attributes the success of the TED model to "a philosophical belief in the importance of openness." He believes there is a whole world of people who are excited by learning and being a part of the creation and spreading of new ideas and original thinking. As he puts it, "We trust the community and the belief in the power of ideas."

I had a clear vision of TEDxMIA as an exposition of the invisible genius I knew existed in Miami. And I knew that the trick was in assembling precisely the right people to facilitate, make presentations, and attend this event. It was my dream to surround myself, in this single gathering, with just the kinds of geniuses who excite and inspire me. But how, exactly, to pull that off? Then, on a flight to D.C., I met the amazing Evelyn Greer, a community leader and major influencer in Miami, and discovered that the stranger in seat 1B was also a TED devotee. Within two weeks of our meeting on that two-hour flight, Evelyn helped to assemble the core group for our event, an eclectic and brilliant bunch that included a green developer, a fund-raiser, a multilingual communications expert, a journalist, and a technologist who worked with me to put together the complex pieces of a simply extraordinary event, one that profoundly affected every individual who attended.

Now, just as you can't eat ice cream every day, you can't expect mind-blowing TED-like experiences every day. Or can you? Here's what I have learned about curating the group experience from participating in TEDGlobal at Oxford and curating TEDxMIA: Every time you put people together, it's an opportunity to invent a new thread of the conversation. And the way to guarantee that that happens is to choose participants carefully, facilitate with intelligence, grace, and precision, and demand nothing less than genius from everyone involved. This can be an exhausting undertaking, but it is as rewarding as anything else I have ever experienced. Today, when I plan a dinner for five or a seminar for fifty, I approach it with just the same respect for the investment each of us is making in the outcome of the gathering. I expect revelation and transformation and the highest-level contributions from myself and everyone else involved. And if there's a chance to squeeze in a little dancing with my group, I do that, too. Living as if every day is TED is one way to up the ante, let me tell you!

PLAYBOOK

You're the Curator

Plan a gathering of five people around a single subject. Select them from inside your tribe and outside your tribe, from different disciplines and different demographics. The one thing they need to have in common is some kind of connection over the subject you propose. For example, you've been bugged lately over the discussion in the news about kids and obesity and want to find a way to make a difference on this subject in your community. What kind of group might you assemble that would gather around this subject for an hour or two, bringing disparate insights, ideas, and experiences to generate a practical local approach to this issue? Don't just call up the usual suspects to participate in a group event like this; be creative and resourceful, think eclectic versus expected. The right chemistry cooking around a provocative subject can expand horizons and innovative solutions before your eyes.

PORTRAIT OF A PRACTICAL GENIUS

One of my all-time favorite examples of what happens when we surround ourselves with genius is the Orpheus Chamber Orchestra, which is based in New York City. What's remarkable about this group is not its superior talent or its exceptional traditional and contemporary repertoire or even the fact that it's been honored with a Grammy Award. What's crazy genius about this orchestra is that it performs without a conductor.

Orpheus was founded in 1972 by the cellist Julian Fifer and a group of musicians who yearned to perform an orchestral repertoire with the self-governing techniques of a chamber music ensemble. By definition, the performance of chamber music calls for a synergy among the musicians that is quite distinct. A traditional chamber music ensemble features a small number of musicians, each playing a different instrument, and generally performs music written specifically for this intimate configuration. One of the few such conductor-less ensembles performing today anywhere in the world, Orpheus promotes an artist-focused approach to making music, rotating musical leadership roles for each work.

"Nobody comes up and stands at a podium doing the traditional 'tap tap tap,' let's begin," an Orpheus administrator, Da Ping Luo explains it. "Instead, facial expressions are shared amongst the musicians and an intense collective energy is created by the whole of the orchestra at the start of a piece as they all self-lead the music together." Each musician is granted the opportunity to influence the interpretation of any given movement without the need or dependency on one person telling him or her what and how to play a piece. The individual genius of each musician, and the trust each invests in the genius of the others, comes together in a singular and original moment of excellence, like a snowflake.

How exciting to imagine creating a brilliant, intimate orchestra of geniuses around you, those who elevate one another's individual genius and create a distinct collective genius together. *This* is the image of surrounding yourself with genius that I would like to inspire your journey.

SUMMING UP

Practical genius takes a village. Living a life of genius is a social, not solitary, endeavor. We are creatures who crave the inspiration, intelligence, motivation, comfort, and good humor of others who are living life at the intersection of what they love and what they do best. To surround ourselves with geniuses, we must:

- Identify the Yodas, the ambassadors, and the online and real-time members of a tribe, including fat brains, who can help amplify your genius.
- Be intentional. Relationships are choices, not accidents. The power of your intention will grow your circle of geniuses.
- Be open and ready to engage with another genius at any time. You are operating on the same frequency, and if you are paying attention, you *will* find each other.
- As a protégé, your job is to be open, receptive, and completely engaged, and to add value to the relationship yourself.
- To build a tribe that feeds, supports, and roots for you, you have to feed, support, and root for them. Be a tireless, generous sharer and connector.

- Avoid one-night stands, amassing followers instead of true believers, and transactional behavior.
- Practice intimacy, share your stories, and move quickly to follow through on the potential of a genius relationship.
- Communication, generosity, and constantly adding value fuel your genius relationships.
- Learn to curate extraordinary group experiences to feed and grow your genius tribe.

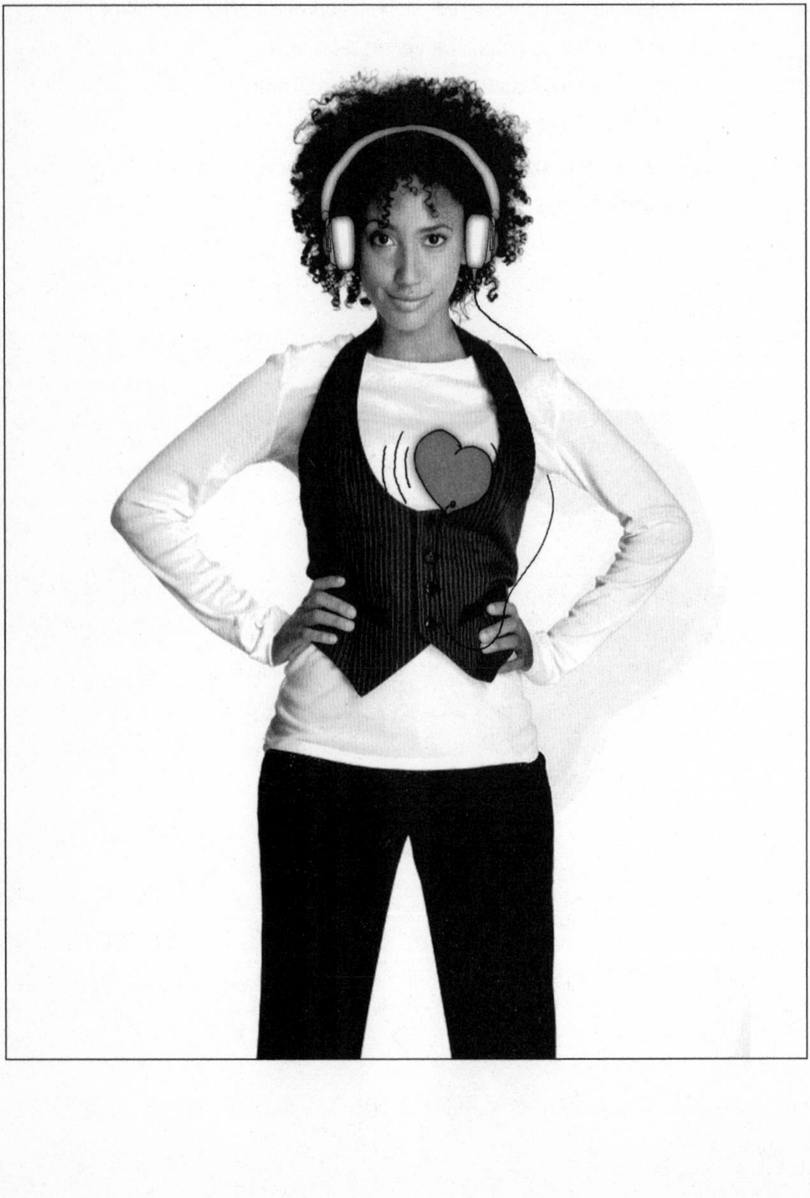

FRANCESCA PRADO

SUSTAIN YOUR GENIUS

Find What Fuels You

The body is an exquisite mystery, an intricate machine of magnificent power and possibility. Yet most of us treat it like a lumpy old sofa. We take it for granted, we ignore its needs, we starve it of all kinds of things—sleep, exercise, nutrients—that are necessary to keep the machine in motion. And as things start to break down or fail (as they inevitably will), we wonder, "Hey, how did that happen? Why me?" Or we chalk it up to aging and begin to brace ourselves for the long slow, increasingly painful march to our Final Destination.

So it is with genius. It's a brilliant, beautiful asset—the essence of you—that is unique and infinitely, exponentially valuable. If you're lucky (or smart) enough to discover it (which is where I hope you are right now!), you ought to treat it like a prizewinning orchid, a rare vintage sports car, a Monet you discovered in your attic. You've got to take care of that baby, or it's not an asset, it's just another dead house-plant, a crap car on cinder blocks, or fodder for your next garage sale.

Sustaining your body is not rocket science (which makes it all the more inexplicable why we don't do it very well). Sustaining your genius isn't rocket science either, but it is an art and involves a surprising variety of components that will feed and help grow big muscles on your genius.

Genius is a lifestyle, a practice that requires a conscious effort to sustain the mind, body, and spirit that get us to that other G-spot—and keep us there. My approach to sustaining genius isn't the usual eat-pray-love stuff. As you might expect, it's a little more practical than that! The way I see it, what we read and watch, the rituals we practice, what we eat, all the things that fill our time—those things represent the *content* of our lives, the content we consume, digest, and turn into the energy that fuels the genius. As with relationships, the content you consume is a choice, and it can either stoke your fire or smother it—you pick.

In order to really shift the paradigm in your life and your work, you have to act upon practical genius as a self-selected lifestyle that sets you up for continued growth, gratification, and ridiculous success. And here's the simple secret of sustaining genius: it's all about choosing the right content for your body, mind, and heart.

I guess you could call this the "tough love" part of our journey. Why? Because if you've come this far and don't understand how important it is to feed this beautiful beast of genius properly—if you think you can keep chowing on Ho Hos when your genius is starving for *mille-feuilles*—well, you're not quite ready to unleash your genius on the world. So let's break this down into pieces.

First, we'll look at your genius mind, where we will explore a radical approach to spending (not managing) your time, which is your greatest energy reserve; gorging on genius stimulants; and the imperative of shutting down. Next, we'll consider the genius body, where we will explore how food, motion, and sleep are critical to active genius.

Finally, we'll look at the genius heart, which will reveal how the mind, body, and heart come together in play, how joy is realized in the "flow state," and how to expand your self-awareness and spend your genius in order to preserve it.

FEED YOUR MIND

Here's a funny truth: time management is a hoax. Billions of dollars a year are spent by well-meaning folks who have an idea that they're not getting enough out of their days and go to great lengths (and expense) to organize their lives, to be more productive, and to figure out the secret of checking off every item on the daily to-do list.

Think about the routines and patterns of your typical day. Are you one of those type As who approach each day with a plan of attack, feeling delicious pangs of gratification with each accomplishment? Is your schedule like a carefully planned military campaign, with every objective supported by a strategy and clever tactics for getting it all done? Or are you more relaxed about how your day unfolds? A little of this, a little of that, but basically just keeping on keeping on, without much to show for your twenty-four hours. As different as these two approaches seem to be, they have one powerfully mistaken thing in common: they assume that time is a tool, like an ax, and the better you wield the tool, the bigger the pile of wood you end up with at the end of the day.

I know this because I've been there. I *was* that person celebrating every task ticked off my many lists, thinking that the tasks represented the important work I needed to accomplish every day if I could only organize myself and manage my time properly. In my mind, ticking off the tasks proved my market value; the more I could do, the more I was worth to the people I worked with, my friends, and my family.

Do you see why this is not a viable or even humane way to look at your time? Attempting to "manage" your time in order to increase your output misses the point of time entirely. It's time itself that has the value, not the millions of tasks and chores and to-dos we try to pull off within it. Time is precious, limited, and the single most important resource supporting your genius. You don't *manage* time, you *spend* it.

Time Matters

Instead of attempting to manage your time focused on output, think about how to *spend* your time focused on feeding your genius. Consider for a moment the act of spending—making a choice to acquire something you have convinced yourself will have value to you, taking out your wallet, carefully counting out your hard-earned cash, handing it over, and finally extracting value out of the purchase itself. Thinking about time that way changes things, doesn't it? And thinking about its being pointed inward instead of outward changes things, too, right?

Somehow, we have gotten into the bad habit of assigning value to the time we manage (our working hours) and looking at the time we spend (after hours, vacations, Sunday mornings) as *free.* The fact is, every minute of the day, awake or asleep, is valuable and free, strictly optional and ready currency. Here's the crux of it: managing time is an organizational pursuit; spending time is an expression of your purpose.

Why do you think vacations are so good at recharging your batteries and reengaging you with your more authentic self? Because you *pick* everything you do on vacation to indulge your passions, your physical desires, your intellectual curiosities. You're much more inclined to say "What the heck" and try a new food or activity or pass an hour doing something you would never do "at home." You're more relaxed and open, you're feeling risk-frisky. (Hang gliding? Hovering over a volcano in a helicopter? Taking a tango class? Why not!) Everything feels like a little treat you're giving yourself.

That's because you are 100 percent in input mode. On vacation, it's all about feeding and indulging and replenishing. You're turning your energy inward, pursuing pleasure, wellness, contemplation, and a little mindful stillness. You're exposing yourself to sights and sounds and experiences that stretch and enrich you. You go home feeling more than just refreshed; you are expanded.

Back at home in your day-to-day, time-managed life, you're in the output mode, turning your energy toward what you think you must produce or accomplish, which tends to sap, deplete, and expend your resources rather than increase them. Routine replaces enrichment; your schedule puts you back to work on tasks, chores, and obligations. Your to-do lists do not include items such as "seek adventure" or "ride bike at twilight." You see why the genius is not having any of this, right?

Three years ago, I realized I had become a slave to the output-oriented way of life, and I made the conscious decision to build my days around what I love first and foremost and to look at the input—the content I consume—as my prioritizing force. I made a commitment to use my natural resources, both soft and hard, to make this shift, and the outcome was more dramatic than I'd imagined. Here's what I learned along the way.

Feed Your Genius First

You know when you're on a plane, about to take off, and the flight attendants are explaining the emergency procedures? I love the part where they tell you to put your own oxygen mask on first before helping someone else. From an emergency procedures standpoint, this is necessary because you're not going to be much help to a child who needs assistance with his mask if you're gasping for air yourself. So it goes with genius. Your primary obligation—to yourself, your colleagues, your friends, and your family—is to take care of your own needs first in order to be most useful and valuable to others.

From a strictly practical perspective, the best way to do this is to feed your genius first. That means spending time on your own edification and growth before you do a single other thing in your day. In other words, don't reach for your BlackBerry first or dive into the chaos of getting the kids off to school before you focus on yourself. Instead, get up an hour early with the purpose of investing in your genius assets—stimulating your curiosity, stretching your intellectual or creative reach, taking a brisk walk around the block to fill your lungs with the fresh air of a new day, listening to music that inspires you, thinking about color or light or anything that interests you that is outside of the "what you do" scope of your day.

My client John Gordon who is the controller and senior vice president of BET Networks, spends this hour in a wonderful way that feeds his genius—and feeds his family, too. John is the classic high-powered executive who also happens to love to cook. So he gets up early every day to experiment with breakfast for his wife and four daughters. He makes porridge, oatmeal, or grits; eggs and bacon; hotcakes or fancy waffles. More than producing all that good food for his girls, though, he is *creating*—writing a symphony, painting a masterpiece, designing an architectural wonder. He teases his kids by saying "Did you know that breakfast eaters score higher on math tests?" But he's dead serious in setting the tone and intention for his own day in a way that stays with him through his last meeting of the day.

A very type-A investment banker I know told me about a very unlikely discovery she made that taught her how to feed her genius first. On her last day in a vacation house she rented one summer, she found a copy of Mevlana Jalaluddin Rumi's classic *Love's Ripening.* This is a woman who carefully avoided poetry and most other literature throughout her extensive education, focusing instead on the math and business courses she knew would get her where she wanted to go. When she found this book, she wasn't any more interested in poetry than she had been in college. But she was fascinated by how worn the book was, with many dog-eared pages and a badly creased spine. She could see that someone (probably several someones) had read it with a great deal of purpose and absorption, and she succumbed to curiosity over what could have so engaged these readers.

She decided to pinch the book and take it home and read it, not in a big gulp the way you read a beach novel but in careful bites every morning after rising, mostly because she was a little embarrassed at what her partner would think when he discovered his hard-charging, career-first wife was suddenly reading love poems! What happened, of course, was that her little dalliance with Rumi on love and friendship, the feminine and the divine—well, it changed her.

It didn't turn her into a poetry lover, by any stretch. But it revealed to her the tremendous power of spending this key bit of time in the day focused on her own growth and understanding, especially through the lens of something so different from anything she had experienced before. She was also surprised by the way that what she read every morning colored and informed her thoughts and energy throughout the day. She noticed that her perspective became more balanced and creative as a result of the exotic little vacation she was taking first thing every morning.

Now this is her habit—she paints for an hour before work, gets through four or five pages of the Proust she's been reading (slowly) in the original French, or loads a shuffle of Brazilian music to listen to on her iPod as she walks the long way to buy her newspaper and latte. She didn't set out to change the quality of her life, although it is likely that it is better than it was before. What she has done is change the way she experiences the whole of her life, the way she sees it every day, by investing in herself this way.

I can't promise swimming with dolphins before your first conference call of the day, but I can promise that focusing on input rather than output and feeding your genius first thing every day may be one of the most permanently transformative adjustments you can make to your life. Where to begin? Look no further than your own journal.

Besides any of the writing or thinking you're working out in your journal, you should be keeping a list of what I call "curiosities," little squibs and dabs of information about music, books, art, food, film—anything, really, that catches your eye or ear and makes you think you might want to know more. This part of my journaling life includes lists of musicians or songs I have read about but have not yet heard; notes about writers and interesting business types I want to investigate; even a recipe for an Andalusian *tortilla de patatas* I want to learn to make.

I refer to these lists and items often, constantly gathering the ingredients that would make a great genius "breakfast." I always have an idea in advance of what I want to spend the time doing; sometimes I explore something for a single day, other times I explore a single subject over the course of a week or more. I also like to keep things like those wonderful Phaidon art books handy; once a quick glance at an Albrecht Dürer painting sent me on a very fun three-day exploration of Dürer's illuminations. The idea is to be in a permanent state of curiosity seeking in order to have a robust menu of choices at the ready for every morning's genius meal.

PLAYBOOK

Make a Menu

Identify three subjects or objects or individuals you know nothing about. Example: science fiction, obelisk, Hank Williams, Sr. Think about how you would attempt to learn more about them. Google's always a good place to start, as is Wikipedia, but the goal is to find an interesting little thread to pull and see where it leads you. So a first look at the history of science fiction reminds you that H. G. Wells and Jules Verne were early pioneers of the genre, but you also learn that Mary Shelley's *Frankenstein* and *The Last Man* are considered definitive models of the form of the science fiction novel. You loved the movie about the summer Mary, her husband, Percy Bysshe Shelley, and Lord Byron spent in Switzerland, where she wrote *Frankenstein*. You read *Frankenstein* in high school, but you've never read *The Last Man*. You order that from the library, and you have a whole week's worth of exploring and expanding to do before you even brush your teeth in the morning! Start with just three curiosities, and you'll be amazed how far they will stretch you.

Establishing this ritual will change the way you experience your day. When you lead with your values, everything that follows has a purpose. It changes your perspective on why and how you're doing your work, caring for your family, or whatever. Over time it creates an extraordinary genius state of grace that causes you to make the choices you know will nurture and sustain you throughout your day.

SUSTAINING PRACTICAL GENIUS PYRAMID

Now Proceed Headfirst Through the Day

After you've set the stage for your day with a strong morning ritual that feeds your genius, do your best to prioritize what immediately follows to utilize and maximize your fresh, engaged brain. Forget racing to your computer to answer meaningless, genius-sapping e-mail. Instead, front load your day with tasks, projects, meetings, or conversations that require analytical ability, such as planning, evaluation, brainstorming, or problem solving. The goal is to prioritize the activities that enable you to use both sides of your brain simultaneously—the left, logical side and the right, creative side—which, of course, means engaging your passions, creative abilities, values, skills, strengths, and expertise. Genius!

This is not just to encourage you to use your energy and best resources early in the day, when you have them, rather than later in the day, when they are depleted. Doing this will actually cause you to *generate* energy and fresh resources that will sustain you throughout the day. Instead of being beat when you turn your attention to your family after work, your engines will be running on a store of energy that will make the end of your day as rewarding and engaging as the start of it.

One trick to this is being careful to address the transactional stuff you need to do *after* you have invested the time you need to in the smart stuff. E-mailing, returning calls, invoicing, anything that falls in the category I call the "housekeeping" of work should happen in the later part of your workday. Making this shift sounds radical, and you may have trouble justifying it to the people you work with. But trust me, if you make this change in the way your day unfolds, everyone in your life will fall into line. You will be profoundly more productive, and the quality of your work will improve. People will be begging to get to work with the "new you" and won't even notice that the price for this privilege is that you don't answer their e-mails until after three!

Be Voracious

Here's where I encourage you to make a pig of yourself. Really. Regardless of the time of day, day of the week, or month of the year, I want you to be a voracious consumer of content. Harking back to my definition of content earlier in this chapter, this refers not just to how you spend your time but what *exactly* you're spending it on. Remember that every bit of content you consume is a choice.

Think of it this way: Are you phoning it in at Ordinary Joe's yoga class? Or do you walk out of Extraordinary Joe's spin class glowing with well-being? Do you eat your sandwich at your desk at work?

Or do you eat it on a park bench watching those awesome percussionists beating the hell out of a bunch of drums? Do you scan the horizon every day for new adventures and possibilities, or do you just double-check the TV listings to be sure you won't miss your episode of *Closer.*

These are choices, people! Every day is filled with dozens of exciting choices most of us simply don't make. Or, to be precise, we make choices, it's just that they're often likely to be the choices that will degenius us (ahem, *Closer*). Things to read, see, listen to, taste, do—they're out there, and they *will* grow your genius.

What I propose is nearly as dramatic in its transformative potential as the feed-your-genius morning ritual: do one thing every day that represents a conscious effort to expose yourself to the extraordinary instead of the ordinary, the profound instead of the pedestrian, the breathtaking instead of the mind-numbing. This is *so* easy to do, and the rewards of this simple effort are monumental.

All it requires is paying attention to what's possible and then doing one thing a day. One thing! Don't just sleepwalk through your morning newspaper; tune your radar to find the one quirky, playful, inspirational, beautiful thing you can see, do, listen to, read, or watch today. Subscribe to blogs or newsletters dedicated to keeping readers apprised of the best of what's up in the world. Or remind yourself of the incredible resources that have been available to you all along—museums, local playhouses, concert halls and houses of worship, schools and universities.

I have one friend who's a committed one-thing-a-dayer. He is great at ferreting out the coolest current doings in his city, as well as accessing ongoing resources. He's also good at spending his time thoughtfully and efficiently in these pursuits. He rarely just eats his lunch; he's always coupling his meal with his outing and often invites others along. When there isn't an *au courant* experience that catches his eye, he makes his way to one of the dozens of galleries in his neighborhood just to "take it in," as he describes it. He also taught me one of his best tricks, to "make a date with art."

PLAYBOOK

Make a Date with Art

Instead of going to a museum and attempting to absorb and digest the whole of it, identify a single piece of art there in which you will invest all of whatever time you have. Take the Museum of Modern Art in New York, for example. Go on the museum's website and find one Mondrian or Matisse or Moore you'd like to have a date with. Do a little research on the piece if you like, or just show up cold and take it in. Spend as much time as you can with the piece, making notes of your impressions or questions or any of the ways in which the piece resonates with you or even disturbs you. Keep a journal of just your dates with art, and over time you will see how your perspective has been made keener by this intimate experience.

You can do this with a piece of art or any single thing on which you would like to truly focus your attention—a building, a particular vista, the evening vespers at a local church or cathedral. Just be fully present and ready to observe and experience every little detail.

I have to say that being a voracious consumer of content has the particular benefit of making you much more aware of how your own work and passions relate to the work and passions of others. The more you see and experience the product of others' genius, the more alive and relevant your own will become.

Shut Down

One of the most valuable lessons I have learned in my journey has been the critical importance of shutting down. I don't mean go into some kind of one-eye-open sleep mode or offline state, I mean *shut down*. This is purposefully closing off the entryways into your consciousness from all the memes and bits and mostly digital detritus that causes what is commonly known as information overload. I never really took shutting down seriously, frankly, thinking that some version of unplugging (i.e., checking the BlackBerry every twenty minutes instead of every five) was a good enough until I got straightened out good by Chris Anderson, the curator of TED, and David Rowan, the editor of *Wired* in the United Kingdom.

"It's important to truly disconnect from time to time. To immerse yourself in nature, to immerse yourself in silence, to breathe, to exercise, to meditate," says Chris. "To do all those things that would allow you to reclaim yourself and to purge some of the clutter and chatter and noise that comes in, because it can become too much. We're natural devourers of information; it's one of the key things that gave our species an edge. But in a world of infinite information, total information abundance, there's a real risk of overload, of information stress, of destructive distraction. It can kill productivity; it can kill relationships."

David Rowan adds, "We're drowning in information, and it's hurting our ability to concentrate. You have to be very disciplined to switch off completely at least once a day. Shutting down allows you to think at a deeper level and provides stillness for this kind of dedicated thinking time. It is then your brain does what it was built to do and magic happens."

On this advice, I began shutting down for a minimum of thirty minutes at the end of every day. This was a tricky one for me to master, but I have to admit, the clearing in my head was kind of amazing and allowed for a kind of authentic engagement with my own thoughts and with my family in a way I had not experienced before. Hint: you need to get everyone behind the shutting-down program. No phone calls, no television, no computer or handhelds. If you're alone, no prob. But tricking a five-year-old into turning off his favorite show so Mommy can shut down isn't easy. So choose your shutdown time wisely, and get buy-in from your crew. I guarantee that you will all feel the difference.

FEED YOUR BODY

Don't worry. I'm not going to try to boss you into eating tofu and birdseed. I am going to boss you into making conscious, genius choices about what you consume, knowing that it makes a difference in the way you work, play, relate to others, sleep, and otherwise attempt to gain pleasure from your life. What you eat and how you use your body aren't about your weight or your waistline; they're about how they give both your head and your heart what they need to produce your genius.

The Care and Feeding of Genius

One of the best ways I have discovered to assess the importance of the content of what we eat is to measure the success of those around me in relationship to their diets. Sometimes I quietly observe the behavior of others, and sometimes I just ask! I'm intensely curious about what fuels each person's genius, and when I see people who are clearly operating in the zone, right at their other G-spot, I try to find out what's on their plate. From a whole range of genius clients, community members, friends, educators, thought leaders, business associates, and all of my genius crew I have learned a common denominator—they eat purposefully.

Wanting to test this theory out in my own life, I began to try to isolate and identify the foods and drinks that really make a difference in my energy, alertness, and engagement. I turned myself into a little lab rat, focused on what each meal and the variety of foods I tended to eat at those meals was actually doing for me. Over time, I discovered that some foods were really putting something in the bank for me—berries in the morning, for example. Nutrition-minded people have been talking about the antioxidant benefits of blueberries and other berries for a while now, and I heard them. But the difference between eating a fistful of blueberries at some point in the day and eating a bowl of blueberries first thing in the morning was noticeable for me. Along with a cup of super green matcha tea, I found I was wonderfully alert, but not in a molto-grande-double-espresso kind of way, more like a just-woke-up-from-the-world's-nicest-nap kind of way. Buddhist monks drink this tea when preparing for twelve-hour meditation sessions, and now I know why. I feel crisp, fed but not weighed down, and ready to get to the smart part of my day. The whole-wheat bagel or bowl of granola or egg-white omelette I had been eating for breakfast for the previous few years probably wasn't hurting me, but they definitely weren't helping me either.

I went through this kind of trial-and-error, remove-and-replace process across most of the foods and drinks I consumed regularly and landed on a pretty tight combination of things that I can count on juicing my genius jets and giving me the energy and mental resources I need throughout the day. For me, it's food like wild salmon, with all those great omega-3 essential fatty acids that are essential for brain function. Or avocados. Like any good Puerto Rican, I love avocados. But I recently discovered that they love me right back, their unsaturated fat contributing to healthy blood flow to the brain and potassium supporting mental function and nerve impulses. It doesn't hurt that I have an awesome hundred-year-old avocado tree in my backyard!

My day is also punctuated with nuts and seeds such as walnuts, almonds, cashews, peanuts, sunflower seeds, sesame seeds, and yes, a little flaxseed that I mix into things here and there. Beans have replaced rice and pasta most of the time, too. And though what feeds a genius truly varies from one to the next, I will go out on a limb and speak for all of us in saying "Genius loves chocolate." Especially really good, really dark chocolate. If you disagree, I don't mind—it's more chocolate for me.

I have a friend who was a lifelong Pop Tarts or Cap'n Crunch for breakfast type, and she had reached a point where she really wanted to replace the eating habits that were holding her back with habits that would boost her genius. Now, there's a reason she's a Pop Tart girl; she's fun and funny, and of course she's eating Pop Tarts, right? Still, how to help her find the way to feed her genius? She thought back to breakfasts she'd loved as a child—in particular, toast with peanut butter and Fluffernutter, of course. She decided to experiment with a genius version of that breakfast, with crunchy toasted sprouted grain bread slathered with a natural (but good-tasting) peanut butter, *sans* the marshmallow Fluff. At first she whined, "It's not the same." But eventually she started to feel the difference between her old genius-busting breakfast habits and this new approach, and she started loving her new peanut butter toast. There is nothing like landing on the combination of foods that lift you rather than hold you back to motivate you to keep testing, trying, moving foods around to see whether they work better early in the day or later, or just moving them out altogether.

On the subject of genius busters, there's one thing we do have in common: the high levels of refined sugar, white flour, trans fats, salt, and a bunch of terrifying additives we've consumed over the years that are now hiding out in every nook and cranny of our bodies, like those creepy sand guys in *Star Wars*, hurt us *all*. They combine to accumulate in our systems and drag us down, slowing our minds, our reflexes, and our muscle recovery, thickening our bodies, and wrecking our sleep. If you want to know what is making you feel bad on any given day, there's a decent chance it's that crap. For me, the real genius busters are alcohol, artificial sweeteners, caffeine, sugary beverages, greasy or processed foods, and the granddaddy of genius-busting grub: white bread.

I'm not preaching, I'm just telling you what we all know to be true. There's a term from the early days of computing, GIGO: garbage in, garbage out. At the time, it meant that a computer, not knowing the difference between bad data input and good data input would process it regardless and produce bad data output. The same goes for what we're talking about here. If you really mean to invest in your genius 100 percent, it's going to take some housekeeping. Eat whatever you want, I mean it. Just eat what you know lifts you up and lets you access the very best of your perfect combination of assets and takes you to—and keeps you at—your other G-spot every day.

PLAYBOOK

Ask a Young Genius

One thing I have learned is that Gen Yers were raised with a different mind-set about food than we were. Notwithstanding the epidemic and epic obesity among children in this country, there's a whole bunch of young people who have been paying attention to information about food as fuel and have adopted an approach to eating that fine-tunes their bodies and their minds. They still know how to party, don't get me wrong, but you can learn a lot from their internal logic about food. Ask a few of your fat brains how they approach food and drink in their lives. Listen for how they describe not just what they eat but when they eat as well as when they go to bed, when they get up, what they do throughout the day to keep the machine running on all cylinders. I guarantee you will learn one incredible thing from them that will change the way you think about this.

A Genius Body in Motion

You know, in the same way time management is a hoax, so is exercise. Exercise is an external, self-imposed prescription for the body, whereas movement is a way of syncing up the body's relationship with the world. Hmmmm . . . which would you choose?

Ironically, I came to this conclusion based on what I learned from a fitness guru named Michael Gonzalez-Wallace. Michael taught me about BDNF (brain-derived neurotrophic factor), a protein that promotes the neuronal growth. Researchers and physiologists have known for a long time that aerobic exercise of any kind increases the production of BDNF and causes the new and preexisting neurons to branch out, join together, and communicate with one another in new ways. When our nerve connections get thicker, we're able to speed up our reasoning processes related to all kinds of things, including problem solving, creativity, learning, memory, and higher thinking. That's why sometimes even just chugging away on a treadmill in the morning, a new idea may occur to you or a solution to a problem that has been keeping you awake will present itself.

This information didn't make me want to run to an aerobics class, despite my obsession with supporting genius. It was Michael's story that got me.

"I played professional basketball in Spain for many years and as a player became obsessed with performance," Michael told me. "Then I went off to college, studied economics, became a banker, and obsessed over performance in relations to numbers. From basketball to economics to banker, I then decided to become a certified professional trainer from the National Academy of Sports of Medicine and became obsessed with the human body."

As a trainer and, frankly, an egghead, Michael quickly realized that his high-level executive clients became easily distracted by traditional exercise and became bored with the simplicity of movements during training sessions. Exploring what he had responded to in his own life, he designed a program that allows his clients to multitask in a way that is similar to what happens when playing basketball, where your strategic mind and your body must engage simultaneously and almost continuously.

"For example, instead of having my clients just do bicep curls, I have them combine a right-arm biceps curl with a left-leg lift, forcing the mind and body to work together to accomplish the movement, coordinating left and right and adding balance to the mix, which provokes the brain. By adding balance and coordination with each strength training movement, they became sharper and stronger. Most interesting, though, was that my clients reported to me that they were becoming more focused outside of the gym.

"After seeing the change with my clients, I reached out to neuroscientist Dr. John H. Martin and he explained that by adding complex moves, balance, and strength training together, I was actually accessing the section of the brain's cerebellum, which is the main headquarters for balance, coordination, and intentional movement. This kind of multitasking—having the brain and body work together for the same goal—represents the connection between motor skills and learning, sharpening your mind, and very effectively and efficiently toning your body simultaneously." By figuring out how to activate the cerebellum when the body is in motion, Michael created what I absolutely believe is a practical genius way to think about our bodies—asking the mind to work along with the body to activate the best we've got, the good stuff, the top-shelf bottles at the Oak Bar.

I loved learning how different kinds of movement trigger different kinds of brain activity. Michael explained, "Gina, what happens when you add additional weight to your body, whether it's holding water bottles or dumbbells, is, your brain goes into this wonderfully productive, complex active mode, trying to figure out what do with the extra weight." Knowing the outcome, if you think about what's possible every time this happens, you'd be brain/body multitasking all day long!

Like life—and genius—I think it's being conscious of the combinations of things—the assets, the vocabulary, the people, the chemistry—that can make us astound ourselves. But you have to be committed to the experimentation this requires, the testing, testing, testing that proves theories and illuminates truths and gives you your Madame Curie moment of genius. To be honest, I love this part. I love playing with what's possible, tinkering with the potential of every single thing. Don't forget that genius is always experimenting.

The Big Sleep

We treat sleep like a bodily function, like burping or pooping. It's *so* not a bodily function. It's as spiritual and critical a state of mind and function of genius as I can think of. I once heard Arianna Huffington say that the way to achieve success was to literally "sleep your way to the top." We all deeply need good-quality sleep and are really missing the potential it can unleash. Arianna learned this simple lesson the hard way after collapsing in her office from exhaustion and breaking a cheekbone.

This isn't about the XX number of hours of sleep you need and REMs and every other clinical thing there is to say about sleep. I'm sure you already know what your optimum sleep margins are—when it's best for you to go to bed, when to get up—yet you probably fight the margins at both ends, all the time. Believe me, I did that for a long time. I'm a natural night owl, yet I know that I get more out of my whole being when I fall into sleep somewhere between ten and eleven at night and get up at six, to get my time alone in the morning before the day breaks loose. I've learned that the lack of the amount of sleep and the correct margins of sleep for your mind and body are critical to my practical genius. All-nighters are for teenagers and club kids. Acknowledge your nature as a creature on the planet—you're a morning person, you're a night person—but identify and honor your optimum margins if you want to realize the full potential of every day.

I ♡ GENIUS

Happiness is one thing; joy is quite another. I'm grateful for happiness, don't get me wrong, but I'm ecstatic when one of those bright, stand-alone moments of joy happens. To me, joy is dessert, the wonderful reward for being open to it, for searching for it, for building a life where joy can happen. It's also one of the best indicators we have that we've truly unleashed the genius in our lives.

And Now We Play

Play is the place in which the mind and heart engage in joyful union that is like a shot of adrenaline. Lots of incredibly accomplished people who disparage exercise engage in play in all its recreational forms, understanding its benefit for body and mind. For one, play is a great way to dissipate stress and lift your spirits and is actually one of your greatest basic abilities as a human being. It's also a naturally social endeavor, so every time you play, you create the potential for genius engagement. Every time. I mean it.

"Play is serious business because it changes people's lives," says the play guru Kevin Carroll. Research has shown that play—particularly unstructured, spontaneous games, as opposed to scheduled activities such as music lessons or football practice—is a powerful force in human development. Whether it's a bike ride, a round of tag with your toddler, flying a kite on a Sunday morning with your family, or shelling alone on a beach, a playful state is *always* a healthy state.

From kindergarten to probably sixth grade, recess was the best part of your day, right? Everyone needs recess, geniuses most of all. Regular recess-style disengagement from the norm and active engagement in play can change your mental, physical, and emotional life if you do it with purpose.

You will be surprised how powerful play can be in the workplace in increasing productivity, creativity, problem solving, team spirit and engagement. The play expert and founder of the National Institute for Play, Dr. Stuart Brown, believes that play is more than just fun and is actually the way we build trust with others, as is the case with all animals. If you need to be reminded how to embrace play, just watch your pets; they are your greatest teachers. Infuse physical or mental play throughout your day, and it doesn't matter whether it's social, imaginative, or designing your dream life with Legos or any other objects—just play.

Go deep inside yourself, where play resides, and know that while you are playing you are actually growing your practical genius. When you are in a play state, you are emotionally and physically engaged as well as cognitively engaged. Play allows you to use your head and heart simultaneously, which in turn allows you to engage the true axis of your practical genius, the source of all your personal power. "Where we may have felt pulled in one direction by the heart and another direction by the head, play can allow us to find a balanced course or a third way," says Dr. Brown.

PLAYBOOK

How Do You Play?

Consider your play history. Explore your past, and see what was your greatest moment of play was. Was it with a specific toy? Was it a sport? Was it at a park or while on vacation? How does your early life experience with play compare with what you consider playtime as an adult? It's important to plumb your play history, and don't be surprised if this small exercise is a profound reality check on the power of play in your life.

Find Your Flow

Have you ever been in a kind of zone while working on something or maybe while practicing an instrument or working on a project where you felt one with your experience, where you were doing it, but learning from it at the same time? Where you were feeding it but it was feeding you, too? This is called "flow," a state where you are so wrapped up in an activity that you actually lose yourself completely in the activity and become one with it. "The" flow guy is Mihaly Csík-szentmihályi (Chick-sent-me-high-ee), who describes flow as the state of operation in which a person in an activity is fully immersed in a feeling of energized focus, full involvement, and success in the process of the activity. According to Csíkszentmihályi, "flow" is completely focused motivation and is the ultimate in harnessing the emotions in the service of performing and learning.

PLAYBOOK

Where's Your Flow?

Try to remember an instance when you were so absorbed and rewarded by what you were doing that you looked up and realized that hours had passed; you got lost in the experience. What were you working on? Was it even work, or was it something else? What time of day was it, early or late? What *kind* of day was it—sunny and bright or cold and dark? Did you produce something during that time? Did you learn something? Did you have a personal revelation? Were you alone or with others? Experiment with time of day, location, and light to try to replicate the circumstances to create an environment for flow.

The more time spent within your "flow," the greater your sense of purpose will become and the more it will motivate you to greater and greater accomplishments and rewards. I have been in the flow many times, sometimes unexpectedly, sometimes as a result of a great deal of focus and effort and passion for the work I was involved in. I have learned that it is a fierce kind of magnet; once you experience this feeling, you constantly hope for all of your experiences to feel this way. All of the many components and triggers of genius are great contributors to this state. So you get there, you taste this satisfaction, you figure out how to stay there. I mean it.

"But only man is truly capable of knowing himself." Socrates knew it, and you should, too. Understanding what distinguishes you from the emu referenced in an earlier chapter is your ability to really "know thyself." Flow often comes from being deeply in tune with oneself. This self-awareness is both the gift and the burden of the human race. I choose the gift.

Self-awareness is achieved by constantly reflecting on your intentions and your actions. It is being aware of your own emotions and how to channel them to achieve what you want from life. Too many of us react to life instead of imposing our intentions on our lives. Awareness of ourselves enables us to be proactive and therefore more in control of where we go.

To be mindful is not to edit this body of self-knowledge but just to accept it—all of it. The good, the bad, the needs-improvement areas, the downright ugly, and, most important, the fun areas in your life that have been neglected. Spend the time on self-understanding so you know what you love, how you want to live, and what you can't live without. Become an expert in you. It's difficult to understand your full potential if you haven't studied yourself.

Carlos Dominguez, a senior vice president and technology evangelist with Cisco, motivates audiences worldwide on the power behind social media and how technology is changing how we communicate and collaborate. Cool job, huh? Well, Carlos didn't come to this place in his life by accident.

Carlos, a passionate advocate for innovation, has always loved speaking, motivating, and activating people, teams, and ideas around innovation, but he really didn't make his own greatest passion his professional priority until a few years ago, after his daughter was diagnosed with leukemia.

"Before my daughter got sick, I was traveling five or seven days a week corunning a business unit for Cisco. I was exhausted, missed a bunch of family functions, and frankly, I had lost a little bit of myself. I was off balance and only about ten percent of my time was spent with family. All of a sudden, my wife and I were in Italy on a vacation, and we received a call that my daughter had fallen ill. We came home, and within forty-eight hours we learned she had leukemia. We battled that new reality for nine long months, and we got through it. After that, it changed me forever.

"I returned to work after my ordeal and attended a meeting with my team, a new generation of leaders doing an incredible job; they had a lot of zest and life for the work and had done some really creative things while I was away. As I watched, I excused myself from the room and knew I wasn't needed, nor would I be returning. In this moment, I transitioned to a second chapter in my life, where my family had to come first, and this self-awareness changed my entire professional and personal experience moving forward.

"I went to my boss to tell him of my intention to retire. But instead, he said, 'Carlos, you should probably do what you do best—inspire others.' Cisco had always used me for presentations at customer events because I was one of the most requested speakers for motivating teams across departments. Thinking about this talent, meshed with my desire to honor my family values and combined with my passion for innovation, I decided to give it a shot and reinvent myself. I guess you can say I was finally acknowledging, after twenty years, my practical genius, and through self-awareness and emotional intelligence I knew this was the right change—the only possibility—for me. It wasn't easy and required a lot of soul-searching and logistical adjustments, but I knew I wanted to do something that could make a meaningful and measurable impact on the business. Since my decision, I have discovered that it's been an incredible asset for me and the company and deeply rewarding. Gina, my life gives me joy."

This is what I learned from Carlos: everywhere assets sit underutilized within a company, a community, a family—especially an asset operating in isolation, in a silo, where you're innovating for the sake of the silo but not for the whole. Well, that sucks! By now you have to know that you really have to leverage everything you've got and access all the expertise you have and never prioritize one area over the other. Carlos could easily have retired to nestle down with his family. Instead he acted upon his own innovative, organic genius, creating a new role for himself based on the whole of who he is. Note to self: self-awareness—it's powerful to connect the unlikely dots, to be the whole of yourself, and realize the product is a whole new and improved way to approach your work and life as one. Now, that's innovation!

PORTRAIT OF A PRACTICAL GENIUS

Dr. Christiane Northrup is internationally known for her empowering approach to women's health and wellness and is a leading proponent of medicine and healing that acknowledges the unity of the mind and body, as well as the powerful role of the human spirit in creating health. Following a career as a practicing physician in obstetrics and gynecology for more than twenty-five years, Dr. Northrup has dedicated herself to helping women (and the men who love them) learn how to flourish on all levels creating health, prosperity, and pleasure in their lives.

When asked why the heart matters so much to genius, Dr. Northrup answered, "We're not a brain on a stick. Genius thrives in a healthy body, and we live in a culture in which we have worshipped the brain, the intellect, the linear and the logical thinker within us. And I will tell you this: emotions always win, even if someone has to drop dead of a heart attack. Emotions always win. Knowing this, I have led my entire life toward 'What is my unique contribution?' And these decisions have been made based on my emotions. What moves me to tears, what inspires me and is right on that edge of joy-filled pain, pain-filled joy—that is what I go for. For example, when I first saw a baby being born, I thought I would fall to the floor weeping from the beauty of it all. And so I have followed that and when it comes to me—intuitively—I'm always really surprised.

"The intellect always wants to believe that it's in control, and it isn't. The spirit is in control. And the spirit is where genius comes from, and spirit resides in the heart. You know we say chance favors the prepared mind and that it takes about ten years to become an expert at anything; ten years of immersing oneself in a field. Now, that's true, and yes, we all love the left-hemisphere kind of rigor, but it takes more than that. I'm a big fan of footnotes and scientific rigor and all the rest of it. But if it is not balanced with this more feminine faith-based receiving, it's worthless because it's exhausting and there's no rest to my sympathetic tone without enough parasympathetic tone."

Dr. Northrup's empathetic ability to make connections between things that aren't necessarily connected is remarkable, and speaking with her is like speaking with someone who has a direct line to the gods. So the next time you want to lead life from the head instead of the heart, think twice about that decision, for the heart and emotions, as Dr. Northrup shared, always win.

SUMMING UP

Practical genius is a self-selected lifestyle, where mind, body, and spirit consume content that provide critical sustenance to your genius. Living this lifestyle isn't about dos and don'ts, it's about making choices that feed you, elevate and expand your experience, and bring your awareness into brilliant detail. Keep these ideas in mind.

- **Time matters.** Input comes before output in the way a genius spends her time.
- **Be voracious.** Greed is good when it comes to purposeful consumption of the product of others' genius.
- **Shut down.** When you learn to unplug, solutions to problems will take shape in your mind, new ideas will reveal themselves, and you will begin to enjoy greater intuitiveness.
- **Feed your body first.** You are what you eat. I'm not kidding.
- **A body in motion.** Big revelation: exercise isn't about your bod, it's about your brain.
- **Sleep.** The world's most underrated stimulant is sleep. Get a lot of it.
- **I ♡ genius.** What moves you, moves you toward genius.
- **Now we play.** It is during the play state that the body, mind, and heart come together harmoniously.
- **Find your flow.** Joy happens at the place where focus, motivation, and engagement intersect.

MARKET YOUR GENIUS

Where the Rubber Meets the Road

It is time to take our journey—our amazing journey of genius growth and discovery—to the transactional level. I know, I know, throughout this exploration, I've been very strict about being nontransactional. That's because it's important to focus on developing your understanding, expression, and growth of your genius in an authentic, deeply practical way, keeping the transactional off the table so that the truth of who you are can reveal itself without that pesky selling stuff compromising everything you've worked so hard to realize. But here we are. You have this asset, this product—your genius. Only an idiot would not be thinking about what to do with that now.

The fact is, I *want* you to market the hell out of it. But I don't want you to market the hell out of *it*. I want you to market the hell out of exactly who you are, which is to say, not a package but the authentic genius essence of you, not a concept but a true-to-life, fire-breathing, boundary-busting, definition-defying, game-changing tour de force that makes you wonder what in the world you were doing before you got to this place. So let's talk about marketing.

I have a confession to make: I spent most of my corporate life as a marketer, and only after resigning from my job as a marketer did I really understand the power of marketing. Yep, I was a global marketer obsessed with the marketing needs of my employer, PR Newswire, but I never gave a thought to the marketing of me.

Why did it take getting off that ride for me to realize the power of marketing myself? I wish I could say I was never afforded the opportunity to learn this, but I was given many opportunities in that job. I chose not to share my whole story, my whole truth, or all my assets because of fear. I had every opportunity to market my values, passions, and soft assets, which were pulling at me 24/7 for a very long time, and instead I stayed quiet, waiting for the right time to present itself. It never came. What came instead was frustration, illness, and regret. Thinking back upon it now, hiding any part of myself in that job was the dumbest professional mistake I ever made.

A year after resigning from PR Newswire, I had breakfast with my former CEO, Charles Gregson, an amazing man with a big heart, who asked me, "Gina, why didn't you let anyone know you had a passion for writing? We could easily have put that passion and obvious talent to better use." "I was waiting for the right time," I replied, acutely aware of how lame that sounded. I worked for PR Newswire for eight years and never once marketed my true self. Instead I did what many of us do: I marketed to them what I thought they wanted me to be.

Today, I am a marketing machine, a genius evangelist who spreads her message with every breath, every step, every gesture. I do it in boardrooms, at tot lots, on planes, and on many a stage without hesitation. It took only a giant leap and some serious thought about what this marketer really knows about marketing genius.

Since the 1960s, we've heard about the "Four Ps" of marketing, the four ingredients of the traditional marketing mix: product, price, place, and promotion. When a company considers launching a product or service, they account for these Ps in order to convince themselves that the launch will succeed. They take them into account after the launch, too, tweaking this P and fine-tuning that one as the market for the product or service grows, matures, and finally declines. This model, or some variation on it, has been the means by which traditional marketers have measured, strategized, and executed for a long, long time—not that there's anything wrong with that!

Here's where we veer wildly off the road, to places that only geniuses can find on routes that only geniuses can use to get to their extraordinary destination. The traditional marketing matrix doesn't work for us. That's because we see things differently.

P IS FOR PARADOX

The truth is that you can forget the traditional Four Ps of marketing and focus on just one, a whole other P: **PARADOX.** One of the all-time best words (and not just because it has an x in it), a paradox is generally defined as a seemingly absurd or self-contradictory statement or proposition that actually contains a truth. A paradox is also often an opinion or statement that is contrary to generally accepted ideas, causing one to consider something in a new light.

So a paradox, by definition, defies conventional wisdom. For the genius, it means that when you decide to integrate and exude the opposing forces within yourself and market the whole, original, fully realized you instead of just piecing out and sharing the parts of you you *think* will matter most to a given audience, well, the whole world opens up for you. By boldly representing the elegant contradictions within yourself, you will actually attract, engage, and grow beyond measure.

Imagine what happens when you market the scholar alongside

the fool. The entrepreneur alongside the philosopher. The conservationist alongside the game designer. The CEO alongside the acoustic guitar player. The break dancer alongside the chess master. The award-winning photographer alongside the "deal closer." You know this rare magic when you see it because it's refreshing and inspiring and speaks to your own contradictions in a loud way. When a genius meets or sits in the audience of another genius who is able to own, project, and employ all his contradictions at once in this way, her spider sense tingles.

That's what I adore about Richard Branson and everything he stands for. Love him or hate him, he accepts and leverages his contradictions without apology. He is a master of paradox and surprises his audience regularly with his seamless authenticity. Without any visible effort, he is who he is with a vengeance, working with his natural design from both heart and mind. When you bring together all the parts of your personal orchestra—the strings, the brass, the woodwinds, the percussion—projecting a singing-in-the-shower *real* you, you make original music for the person on the receiving end. Branson does that in spades—and see where it got him!

This is what you need to understand about why you don't need the Four Ps of marketing and all you need is the One P: the One P, the paradox of you, *is* the product, it *is* the price, it *is* the place, and it *is* the promotion of your product, all of it, it's you, it's your genius.

Here's the deal. The paradox of you—your other G-spot, where the whole of you is realized—also activates your potential from a transactional standpoint. Obviously it's what you have to sell (product); it boldly and unconventionally presents itself to establish its value in the marketplace (price); it makes itself available in venues real and virtual in an eclectic, organic, and highly commercial way (place); and it represents a whole world of opportunity for promotion, including some, all, or none of the standard elements of promotion (advertising, public relations, personal selling, and sales promotion).

Generally a company does a massive analysis of the Four Ps before deciding to introduce a product or service into the marketplace. You, on the other hand, need only strategize how to engage with your audience authentically on the basis of your paradox.

Contrast this to the popular concept of personal branding. Rooted in Al Ries and Jack Trout's 1981 book, *Positioning: The Battle for Your Mind,* and later brought into widespread discussion by Tom Peters, the idea that one could position and package oneself like a bar of soap was compelling. You're not just the accountant, you're the accountant who never makes a mistake. You're not just a sales rep, you're the closer. Add to that a makeover to your whole "look"—how you dress, your materials, and so on—and you're *the* bar of soap, baby.

I don't know about you, but I don't really want to be a bar of soap. I don't even want to be *the* bar of soap. I don't want to be one of many in my field scratching and scrambling to distinguish myself, marketing myself madly in the traditional ways most folks know how to turn down and tune out. I don't want to be in a constant state of striving to "be somebody," when who I am right now, where I am right now, is my greatest asset.

Here is the wonderful, free-fall, put-yourself-out-there approach to marketing your genius: You take the sweet spot of genius you've identified, the place where your hard and soft assets meet. You add the expression of your genius, the story you tell that introduces others to that sweet spot. Juice that with the shot of B12 you get from a crew of genius mentors, ambassadors, fat brains, and tribe and all the ways you stoke and provoke your genius mind, body, and heart every day. Now point yourself out toward the world, and live it hard.

Think about it: You've stripped away artifice and conformity, convention and expectation. You are right there at the heightened state of your own power, projecting and distributing your genius naturally as you interact with colleagues, clients, friends, family, and perfect strangers. You're authentic, transparent, and fully engaged. Your paradox—the wonderful, powerful contradictions that make up your genius—presents the ideal selling proposition. What you are is a perfect magnet for exactly the work, people, environment, and experience you want to have in your life.

Here's how it has worked for me: instead of shying away from my paradox—which is a bit of badass meets graceful integrity—I have always accepted my contradictions as a cultured woman with real street smarts who can win the game whether it's played on Wall Street or Main Street.

I walk through life with one foot in a four-inch heel and the other in a combat boot. I'm smart yet edgy, nurturing yet candid, traditional yet rebellious, sexually charged yet driven by deep core values. Think old-school mother meets cultural modernist; ideation freak meets focused strategist; ghetto scholar meets spiritual intuitive; daydreamy ocean lover meets obsessive book collector. Every day is a surprise because I don't know how to censor or edit myself.

I have always led with my paradox, kicked down doors with it, and taken great joy in it. As a result, my paradox has always attracted the right clients, partners, and tribe in my life, people who not only "get" me but are highly motivated by my provocative transparency, the what-you-see-is-what-you-get approach that kind of blows people away. By humbly but boldly exposing all of who I am, I send a signal to my prospective audience that they, too, can safely and fully expose themselves, and the business of engaging together begins.

In this very naked, natural, active state of just being, the genius markets itself without marketing itself. To be precise, your genius is broadcast on all frequencies and the correct audience for your genius responds, making its way into your life from all points of engagement. When you live and leverage your paradox, you present a unique, authentic product that naturally long-tails its way into the marketplace.

Take Traci Fenton, one of my favorite examples of marketing genius by living the paradox out loud. As a senior in college, Traci was the director of a student-run public affairs conference on democracy, which she had come to believe was the best way for people to realize their full potential, not just politically and collectively but personally and individually. After the conference, she spent her last college quarter studying in Indonesia, at the time then-President Suharto was overthrown. The violent, bloody experience, seeing firsthand what it was not to live in a free and democratic environment, affected her deeply.

She returned to the United States and got her first "real" job with a Fortune 500 company, excited to make her mark. Soon after, though, her wide-eyed hopes were dashed when she realized the workplace was one of the most undemocratic environments in which one could find oneself. "After spending the last year of my life studying democracy, my new workplace was a perfect contrast to the ideals I'd come to love and live. I knew I couldn't stay in such a toxic, dehumanizing environment for the next forty years, and I didn't think anyone else should either."

Leading with her genius—her values and passions, her skills and expertise—Traci spent the next decade traveling the world researching democracy, engaging and interacting with thought leaders in organizational development and democratic management. "My driving question was, how can the principles of democracy be applied in the workplace in a way that benefits the people, the bottom line, and the world?" Her organization, WorldBlu, was born of some of the answers to that question and is now working in fifty countries around the world to design, develop, and support successful democratic organizations, companies committed to demonstrating democratic values and behavior in the workplace.

Traci didn't hire a branding firm or a consultant or a buzz agent to present her proposition to the world. She passionately and purposefully told her genius story, she lived and proved her values, she built a passionate tribe around her genius—folks like Tony Hsieh, the CEO of Zappos, and Vineet Nayar of HCL Technologies—that helps to grow WorldBlu's reach every day.

Traci is a brilliant, creative mind—someone who could develop and describe this big, thinky concept but who could also envision and execute the precise logistics to make it happen on a practical level. What I love about her is that she didn't wander around corporate America miserably for ten or twenty years before turning to her purpose in life, the way so many of us do. She was fully baked right out of college and dived right into her genius destiny, her paradox leading the way. She also didn't putz around trying to position her vision, package her program, or get buy-in from marketing partners. She just did it. She lives it first, sells it later. See how that works?

PLAYBOOK

What's Your Paradox?

The word "paradox" comes from the Greek *paradoxos,* which means "contrary to opinion or expectation." What about you is contrary or defies expectations? What are the dynamically dueling aspects of your nature that make you an original? Here's my paradox: Mother, rebel, advocate, strategist, writer, urbanite, corporate provocateur. What's yours?

If you're really paying attention, you'll notice that paradox also impacts organizations lately, prompted in part by the technocentric reality of our lives. Companies are beginning to realize that assets that used to be considered opposing forces (IT left-brainers and marketer right-brainers, for example) are being fused instead of separated, creating a new kind of fully realized organism—in this particular example, someone called a marketing technologist. Imagine the promise of a company filled with whole—not incomplete or pigeonholed—people who naturally integrate their energy and effort instead of operating side by side in parallel play, to borrow a compelling term from the child development field. What a tremendous mind-set shift this represents. This is where the market value of genius establishes itself.

VIVA LA DIFFERENCIA!

Marketing your genius is all about acknowledging and leveraging what is unique within your paradox. It's about isolating and identifying what differentiates you, which is, of course, your particular genius. That's why you need to think of your genius as a premium asset rather than a commodity.

Gasoline is a commodity; its price fluctuates based on supply and demand, not on the quality or features of the product. You don't know or care where it comes from, just so long as you can get it when you need it. A luxury car, on the other hand, is a product that is entirely distinguished by its points of differentiation, the features that set one car apart from another and establish relative value in the mind of the consumer. A luxury car is defined by its distinctive features, high value, and superior quality—the premium aspect that transforms it from a product into an asset and attracts just the consumers who can appreciate, benefit from, or leverage that particular asset. That's your genius, the premium asset.

The Commodity	The Premium Asset
Widely available	Exclusive
Standard	Uniquely tailored and selective
Low status	High quality
Undifferentiated	Versatility and precise differentiation

The most distinctive global brands—Apple, Google, Pixar, Sony, Virgin—became what they are today because of deliberate efforts to set themselves apart as a premium asset, not just another product or service in a crowded marketplace. This kind of differentiation creates perceived value and demand, attracts interest, and provides stimulation of and energy around the brand. And the authenticity and consistency of the consumer experience close deals, seal relationships, and hold the brand accountable to its own standards.

A very distinct vocabulary and approach are required when you start marketing how different you are as a premium asset. When I discuss this with my executive clients, they often worry out loud that they don't have any authentic differences to celebrate. They all wonder, "Is anyone really truly unique and different?" The answer is, unequivocally, absolutely yes. There is no one like you! You have come all this way on your genius journey—by now you know exactly what you have that no one else does. The marketing of your genius requires you to present those points of differentiation, in everything you say and do, so that the value of your genius is obvious.

YOU AND YOUR AUDIENCE

The market for your genius—the audience to whom you broadcast, with whom you engage, and to whom you add value—isn't vast or infinite. Ultimately, your audience is your tribe and therefore is carefully curated. You're not promoting your genius to a mass market, you're building a market for your genius one by one.

The corporate and personal branding expert William Arruda told me, "It's not about becoming famous; it's about being selectively famous with just that small set of people who need to know you." The biggest mistake he sees many people make when it comes to targeting an audience is that many times they ignore the ecosystem that already exists within their own communities and personal networks. So start small, think niche, and don't ignore the tribe you have already established.

In the early days of his start-up consultancy, William said, he missed having colleagues. To conquer the loneliness, he started a personal branding certification program as a way of building an ecosystem for himself, and today he enjoys the camaraderie of more than two thousand strategists, including myself. "Engage your ecosystem with a concise, clear message, and they will spread your message for you and with you," he advises. The people you sell to are the same people who sell you—your values, goals, and satisfaction are in sync.

PLAYBOOK

Visualize Your Audience

Think about the people you have worked with who have come to represent the gold standard for you. Think of clients, partners, colleagues, bosses, vendors, interns—anyone with whom you have worked who taught you something important, made the experience rewarding and memorable, or in any way changed the way you do what you do and for whom you have done the same. By now you should be able see the common thread. These are the people with whom you created value. This is what your audience looks like—people who are attracted to your paradox and want to leverage your genius.

ATTRACT. ENGAGE. GROW.

Marketers love to measure. They're crazy for all the analytics and metrics that help them account for the performance and success of their marketing initiatives and maximize the return on investment in marketing and promotion. That means dollars. The genius measure of marketing performance is based on three indicators: attraction, engagement, and growth. What makes this approach to measurement different from traditional marketing is that it's as much focused on your own satisfaction as it is on that of your audience. It's both a value-driven mind-set and a way to test whether what you're doing is producing the results you want.

It is a lens through which you observe and tweak your own experience. It's also an action plan in which you establish specific goals, a strategy to meet those goals, and tactics that execute the strategy.

For example, say you were a classical pianist in college and are now a corporate executive. As a genius who has integrated the creative with the strategic and who's ready to promote the paradox, one way to attract an audience for your genius is to perform for small audiences. To engage an audience of genius, you might join an ensemble. And to grow your audience, you might join an association of pianists, which will feed your genius while simultaneously growing your tribe.

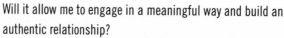

PLAYBOOK

Three Questions

To assess the potential of a strategy or tactic, ask yourself these three questions:

 Will it attract my niche audience?

 Will it allow me to engage in a meaningful way and build an authentic relationship?

Will I grow as my audience grows?

Attract

Consider for a moment the universal law of attraction, which posits that "like attracts like." This belief suggests that you attract into your life what you project to the universe. The genius corollary to this law is that the attraction you seek begins and ends with your intentions. Whether it's positive visibility, new business opportunities, or the positive perception of your tribe, you will experience the outcome that you visualize and intend.

If your attraction intentions are not really intentions at all but just superficial desires driven by your ego, you will end up with a bragging campaign rather than a branding campaign. Lots of companies make this mistake, foolishly believing that promoting how great they are will attract customers to their brand. There was a day when communication was less complex and consumers were less sophisticated and simply yelling "We're number one!" was enough to reach and convince a broad audience. Those days are gone. Today, the winners are companies that attract by serving their audience and answering their needs. The golden rule of attraction is that it's always about serving a need beyond yourself. It's give, not take; offer, don't reach. It's a mindful, value-driven approach versus a transactional approach, and yes, it's measureable.

For example, when I set out to attract like minds, I lead with the question "What can I do to help you?" The genuine expression of generosity and service of your tribe never fails to bring the audience you seek close to you. This is the kind of attraction that builds success upon success and establishes a pattern of abundance in your life. When you offer every expression of genius as a gift—whether it is through acts of service, meaningful storytelling, or tooting the horn of another genius—the result is always, always, always positive. Better-you positive, better-world positive, and dollar positive. Even the marketers would be happy with that outcome!

The Heart Always Wins

Dr. Northrup was right—the heart always wins. One company that knows a thing or two about attracting and marketing from the heart is Avon Products. Although I was with Avon for only two short years as a manager, it was there that I learned firsthand that if you lead from the heart, you can actually drive revenue growth exponentially while also changing people's lives. Avon may be the world's best example of what happens when you service the needs and encourage the aspirations of your audience. With more than $10 billion in annual revenue, Avon markets to women in more than a hundred countries through approximately 6.2 million active independent Avon sales representatives and grows steadily even during a down economy because they never take their eye off who their audience is and what she needs.

Avon Vice President Joe Billone explained that the spirit of service starts inside the company and radiates out to Avon's audience. "Leadership is everything, and Andrea Jung, Avon's CEO, knows how to lead from the heart. People will always follow the heart much more readily than they will follow orders, and when you work with a brilliant mind who is directing the company from her heart and soul, the following on every level grows."

A true practical genius, Joe is a former Broadway dancer and choreographer who leverages his genius by directing global recognition and motivation efforts, including the recent launch of Avon Voices—a global online singing talent search for women and a songwriting competition for men and women in celebration of the company's 125th anniversary. The program has invited people from sixty-two countries, along with independent sales representatives, to join a global music competition with a panel of judges including music industry leaders such as the Black-Eyed Peas' Fergie and the legendary songwriter Diane Warren. "It's our goal to help raise women up through beauty, inspiration, and song, and we know that music is its own pheromone and really speaks to the heart," said Joe.

The service thread of this campaign extends from the company through the audience and out into the world, as music is made available for digital download, with a percentage of the proceeds supporting the Avon Foundation for Women's global campaign to end violence against women and girls. To date, Avon global philanthropy has raised and awarded more than $30 million directed to domestic and gender violence awareness, education, direct services, and prevention programs. What an incredible paradox—the world's most famous beauty company tackling the ugly reality of domestic and gender violence. It really doesn't get more genius than that.

What I learned from Avon about attracting an audience:

 Attraction has nothing to do with you and everything to do with serving your audience's needs and aspirations.

Lead from the heart, and your audience will follow.

Don't just talk the talk; create a movement around the message with your audience leading the way.

Engage

You're attracting the audience you care about; now how can you involve them in your life and work the way you want to? When it comes to engagement, it's about relationships not marketing. There's no push, no pull, just the establishment of a real and permanent connection with your audience through the relationship. One of the most effective ways to make that connection is to engage over a cause.

Throughout my life I've discovered that the value of community work, volunteerism, and civic involvement goes way beyond do good/feel good. Cause-related alignment can produce life-changing relationships, rewards, and outcomes that will astonish and surprise you, as well as opportunities to engage your audience in a uniquely intimate way. Smart companies have figured out the power behind cause-related marketing, but what interests and inspires me is how it plays out one relationship at a time. Some of the most influential and emotionally rewarding relationships in my network have come out of my volunteer work, as was the case in putting on TEDxMIA. It's the passion behind the work that creates the bond; it's how well you engage and ignite the genius in each other that makes the bond work for you.

I like Heide Gardner's story. Heide is the highest ranking and first African-American officer at the Interpublic Group, a global leader of advertising and marketing services with more than forty thousand employees in all major world markets. Heide, a true service leader, built her genius brand as an African-American marketing and media pioneer, first as a volunteer for a midnight basketball league effort in Glen Arden, Maryland, which a family friend, G. Van Standifer, founded in the hopes of getting young African-American men off the streets at night. In the effort to support his vision, Heide capitalized on the obvious marketing and educational opportunity for the league. Instead of just opening a recreation center for African-American males to play basketball at night, which she doubted corporations would support, she designed a program where young men could take classes at a few local trade schools on some nights and play ball on the other nights. That turned the fledgling program into a cause around which a myriad team of talented and motivated individuals engaged. Smart publicity campaigns and celebrity coach efforts drew national attention to the program, which was awarded President George H. W. Bush's Daily Point of Light Award.

It was Heide's passion as a volunteer leading this charge that inspired one of her sponsors, Coca-Cola Enterprises, to offer her her next career opportunity working on marketing and community relations promotional campaigns. Her unique ability to synthesize and apply learning across a variety of disciplines and her "court sense" catapulted her success, which was first seeded with service and volunteerism.

Doors continued to fly open for Heide, including a leadership role with the American Advertising Federation, where she helped create the Mosaic Center, whose mission is to leverage multicultural talent and ideas. Within this role she realized, for the first time, that her career was making sense to her. I consider that moment to be Heide's practical genius revelation. When she finally brought both her soft and hard assets into play, she found herself working side by side with advertising industry icons such as Tom Burrell, Caroline Jones, Byron Lewis, Bob Wehling, Andrea Alstrup, David Bell, and Vince Cullers to create principles and best practices on diversity and multicultural marketing for the ad industry. Recognized by the White House once again, this time she found herself standing in the Oval Office while President Bill Clinton signed an executive order on contracting for minority-owned businesses and cited in support of the Mosaic Principles.

Eventually Heide joined the Interpublic Group and was the first African-American officer at IPG. When you are serving the higher good, it always leads to personal reward and fulfillment. "Service leadership is what landed me where I am today," says Heide. "It was through my passion, creativity, and service work that I came upon a synthesis of rich life experiences and opportunities. And my greatest opportunities have often started out as unpaid roles from the heart."

What I learned from Heide about engaging over a cause:

- Pick your cause the way you pick your underwear; it must fit comfortably.
- Select organizations and causes that are in alignment with both your soft and hard assets.
- Partner and collaborate with like-minded folks.
- Remember, there is important work to be done through genius engagement at all times, in all places. It can be right on your own doorstep or halfway around the world.

Grow

Here's where I really split off from the mainstream marketers. They want numbers; I want a singular, personal, expandable genius experience. Your own mental, emotional, or spiritual growth must be your marketing imperative as you set out to grow your tribe. If you focus on expanding your multidimensional life experiences, you will grow a tribe and audience of teachers, inspirers, and contributors who share your values and will help to establish and grow your value in the marketplace.

Develop your visibility and mind share with the particular audience you seek by investing all of your genius assets in the relationships that stimulate your own growth. You don't want an audience that reaches far and wide; you want the one that is narrow but deep.

BROADCAST YOUR GENIUS

Never before has it been so easy and inexpensive to share your genius and grow your tribe in such a short amount of time. Today technology is your revolutionary marketing partner. Before long, we will all be communicating simultaneously within three worlds—the face-to-face, real-time world; the online virtual world; and the omniverse, which is the merged real- and virtual-world experience where your real and online identities mesh.

When I try to inspire some of my clients to consider their identities in relation to these growing trends, some still dismiss them out of fear of transparency or by copping the too-busy excuse. "Gina, I don't have the time for social media," one client said. Guess what? This is no longer just an option you can choose from a menu of possible tools. Modernism has spoken, and this multidimensional reality influences your potential impact. If you use the tools well, you will explode your impact. If you ignore the tools, you will be a genius tree falling in the forest. Sounds sad, doesn't it?

Here are the three reasons why you must master social media: (1) Together, they are the most cost-effective, efficient platform with which to build and distribute your insights, messages, and stories. (2) You really can't grow and spread your genius without social interaction, and social media are now a full-blown feature of contemporary social interaction. (3) They will become your teacher. Every practical genius needs teachers, trailblazers, and innovators to expose him or her to what is happening at the fringes.

Ask yourself right now: are you engaged, are you watching with curiosity from the sidelines, or are you ignoring the reality out of fear? The camp in which you sit will determine your relevance in the marketplace. If you're already in the swim, ramp it up with more exploration, more communication, more engagement. If you're sidelining, please dive in *right now*. Find someone in your genius universe who is fluent in this world to teach you the simple strokes that will get you started. And if you're ignoring it, you had better get used to the world ignoring you.

Broadcasting your genius without the help of the social media is not an option for the practical genius because it's a one-dimensional, dispassionate, disinterested, impractical way to approach your experience. I genuinely believe that it's your obligation to be representing your genius in the social media in order to fully engage with your audience.

One rule for online engagement: share your genius. Building relationships and leveraging your assets online should always be about sharing new knowledge with your tribe. I make a point of sharing what I learn from my experience and personal explorations—especially insights from my early-morning genius "breakfasts." I know that the people who are already in my tribe or whom I want to attract to my tribe are hungry for the same kinds of unexpected insights that I am, whether from a video interview, a link to an article, a quote from another blogger, or just an interesting piece of information that surprises or excites me. I refer to those as my "catch of the day." I fish for something to wow me in my RSS feeds and elsewhere. If nothing excites or inspires me, I don't share that day.

This leads to my second rule for geniuses in the online universe: don't post messages or comments or tweet just because. Meaningless chitchat is a two-way time suck that depletes genius. Broadcast value-add information or insight or nothing at all. If what you are sharing isn't a genuine "lightbulb" for you, it won't be for your audience either. Remember, social media engagement is all about sharing new information, having authentic conversations, and attracting other ideas to dance with yours. That's how you grow both yourself and your audience.

There is a collective online consciousness that wants you to be a part of it. You will know you are in your zone online when you engage, contribute to, and collaborate with others with all your forms of content and visuals. Think of this as genius-to-genius sharing, or, as the author Matt Ridley describes it, "when ideas have sex." This is what happens online when ideas come together to mesh and expand, deepen and spread. Contributing in this intricately interactive and circular fashion is a unique collaborative experience, probably a little like tripping in the sixties but madly transformative when something comes of it.

PORTRAIT OF A PRACTICAL GENIUS

Frank Cooper III is the senior vice president and chief consumer engagement officer of PepsiCo. Named one of *Fast Company's* top creatives of 2010, Frank is charged with leading the development of new consumer engagement.

Frank discovered his genius axis as an undergraduate at University of California at Berkeley, studying economic analysis and rhetoric. After graduating from Harvard Law School, Frank began crafting his legacy at Motown Records and Def Jam Recordings before landing at PepsiCo. A true example of an executive living his paradox, Frank plays his guitar daily and is also an avid gamer and a major pioneer in social media. Speaking with him was a lesson in what's possible when what we know about ourselves intersects with what's possible in the digital universe.

Frank created a campaign called DEWmocracy, where he tapped the collective intelligence of Mountain Dew fans—PepsiCo's most passionate consumers—to help write a new chapter in the beverage's history. Based on Mountain Dew's DIY persona, Frank launched a campaign to leverage the concept of thriving outside the mainstream, which was a bit radical for a company like PepsiCo. Knowing he had to listen to his creative instincts, Frank consulted with one of his genius tribe, the actor and director Forest Whitaker, and together they set out to create a virtual world within which Dew fans could actually create a new Mountain Dew flavor. That was the birth of DEWmocracy, which leveraged all sorts of things from social media tools to video-gaming logic to crowdsourcing.

"The campaign allowed ordinary people to create three new beverages, including the names, the packaging, and the ad campaign. We didn't create them; they did," Frank said. "What started out as an experiment based on the belief that within each person there is creativity and within the collective there is more creativity resulted in a profound opportunity to engage with the people we care most about. It was the most successful limited-time product offering in PepsiCo history, with the sale of seventeen million cases in twelve weeks."

This is a great example of engaging the power of the tribe to stimulate growth. By taking a risk and allowing the tribe to innovate on the company's behalf, both the brand and the tribe experienced a profound opportunity to attract, engage, and grow.

SUMMING UP

Marketing genius ain't your father's marketing. It calls for a whole new perspective on who's selling what to whom. And it's where the rubber meets the road on living your practical genius.

 P's for "paradox." Embrace the beautiful opposing forces within you, and exude the whole of your identity without apology. It is when you express the great truth of the whole that marketing becomes effortless.

 Bet on your differences. Identify your points of differentiation (PODs) within yourself, and leverage them as your greatest competitive advantages.

Know your audience. You can't be all things to all people, but you can be everything that matters to a key few. Identify your niche, focus on each and every relationship in a meaningful way, and know exactly what makes that particular audience tick.

Attract. To attract the audience you seek, serve its needs and aspirations. "How can I help you?" is the most powerful marketing tool in your toolbox.

Engage. You've got their attention, now build the relationships you want on a foundation of aligned interests and shared passions.

Grow. Expand your own experience to expand your audience. You grow, your audience grows.

Broadcast your genius. You've mastered the face-to-face and the heart-to-heart. Now unleash the power of the social media to make your genius current, relevant, and fueled by the best the genius universe has to offer.

EPILOGUE: A CALL TO GENIUS

Back to the Beginning

Here you are, all fat and happy, enjoying the hell out of your other G-spot, aren't you? That's nice, but I didn't write this book for *you*, I wrote it for *us*. The real power of practical genius will be fully realized only when it goes beyond what it does for *you* and becomes the monster movement of *we* that it was meant to be.

My name is Gina, and I'm here to recruit you.

Enough with the conformity—on with the rebellion. Enough with the mediocrity—on to excellence. Enough with short-lived transactional hookups—on to lifelong relationships with teachers, fat brains, Yodas, fellow geniuses, and future geniuses that create and compound true value in the world in which we want to live and work. Enough with the de-genius diet—on to a mind, body, and spirit richly fed.

Living life as a practical genius is a choice. It's a conscious choice to be a childlike learner, a curious explorer, a paradox, a guru. It's the choice to accept your contradictions, spread your ideas, and join the other geniuses living at the fringes, where my genius movement is happening as you read this.

This genius life is an experiment. As bossy as I have been while guiding you on this journey, by now you know that there's no right or wrong way to do this. When the dormant dynamic ingredients within you come alive and mesh, what you love becomes what you're good at, what you're good at is what you love, and the unique and unlikely dots of your life connect.

Self-innovation is at your fingertips. Collective innovation is, too. When all our genius assets are engaged and when geniuses are engaged with one another, things change. Genius loves company, but it also has a passport. It travels and spreads and explores uncharted territory and unbeaten paths.

You know a genius when you see one. You know when you see her in the mirror, or standing next to you at a party, or sitting next to you on a train. The power of one practical genius is mighty. The potential of two is a movement.

Join the movement at www.practicalgenius.com.

ACKNOWLEDGMENTS

It really does take a village to actualize a dream, and this book couldn't have happened without the minds and hearts of so many.

THANK YOU, FAMILY!

First and foremost is the wonderful family that surrounds me—my amazing husband, Stephen, whose unconditional support and sacrifice allows me to accomplish the unthinkable; my son, Lucas, whose pure spirit fuels my passion and joy for life; my mom, Juanita Quintana, for being the first to believe in my genius; my dad, Al Amaro, for nourishing me throughout this journey with support and home-cooked meals; my stepmom, Melba Olmeda Amaro, for smiling upon my every word with pure appreciation for the message; my incredible brother, Julian Javier, who keeps the art within me alive; my grandparents Clemente, Frances, and Jovita, whose spiritual guidance enfolds me; and my aunts and uncles, for their loving warmth, thank you!

THANK YOU, YODAS!

Yodas are priceless! Thanks for having my back on this not-so-crazy idea: Sheila Wellington, Kevin Carroll, Daniel Pink, and Melissa Bradley.

THANK YOU, AMBASSADORS!

This tribe of generous givers whom I adore has helped me beyond measure: Katina Rojas Joy, my emotional venture capitalist; David Taggart and Dan Stav; to my amazing assistant, Toma Rusk, who keeps me sane and to my comrades and brilliant TEDxMIA family for igniting a genius movement in Miami when many said it was impossible.

THANK YOU, FAT BRAINS!

To Dan Lack, my MBM entrepreneurial tribe, and my twenty-something mentors—the "fat brains" in my life—thanks for keeping it real with me.

THANK YOU, TRIBE!

To Gina Benning and Ivan Moore, the muses whose insights helped set me free from a life of conformity, thank you. To Dr. Gaston, my acupuncturist, for keeping me healthy throughout this rigorous process. To Tonya Evens, Michelle Minguez Moore, and Adriana Comellas-Macretti for always having my back. To the students and library staff at the Herbert Library at Florida International University, where I camped out for all those months, thanks for offering a supportive writer's cave for me.

THANK YOU, LITERARY GENIUSES!

Finally, this book would have never seen the light of day if it weren't for Karen Watts, my literary agent and editor and the left side of my brain. Karen, you complete me and I love you dearly. And last but not least, Michelle, Stacy, Trish, and my extended Touchstone/Simon & Schuster family—thanks for believing and participating in this movement from the heart.

INDEX

ABOUT THE AUTHOR

Gina is the president of Genuine Insights, Inc., a contemporary professional development and training practice whose mission is to leverage the genius within every individual and organization. Gina spoke on the subject of genius at the TEDGlobal 2010 conference at Oxford University in Oxford, England.

Gina has been a guest lecturer, trainer, and strategist for organizations including Merck Co., BET Networks, the Interpublic Group, the U.S. Department of Agriculture, and the Stern School of Business at New York University among many others. She is the curator of TEDxMIA, an independent movement to spread genius in southern Florida. Before launching her own practice, Gina held management positions at Fortune 500 companies including Avon Products and PR Newswire, where she was responsible for spearheading multicultural and international marketing efforts.

A native New Yorker, Gina graduated with a bachelor's degree in English literature from Binghamton University and is a National Urban Fellow holding a master's degree in public administration from Baruch College in New York City. She now lives in Miami with her husband and son.